OPPORTUNITIES

in

Laser Technology Careers

OPPORTUNITIES

in

Laser Technology Careers

REVISED EDITION

JAN BONE

New York   Chicago   San Francisco   Lisbon   London   Madrid   Mexico City
Milan   New Delhi   San Juan   Seoul   Singapore   Sydney   Toronto

Library of Congress Cataloging-in-Publication Data

Bone, Jan.
    Opportunities in laser technology careers, rev. ed. / by Jan Bone. — 2nd ed.
      p.   cm.
    ISBN 0-07-149309-3 (alk. paper)
    1. Laser industry—Vocational guidance.   I. Title.

  TA1677.B66   2008
  621.36'6023—dc22   2007047007

1 2 3 4 5 6 7 8 9 10 11 12 13 14 15 16 17 18 19 20 DOC/DOC 0 9 8

ISBN 978-0-07-149309-3
MHID   0-07-149309-3

Interior design by Rattray Design

McGraw-Hill books are available at special quantity discounts to use as premiums and sales promotions or for use in corporate training programs. To contact a representative, please visit the Contact Us pages at www.mhprofessional.com.

This book is printed on acid-free paper.

CONTENTS

FOREWORD

I T TAKES COURAGE to work on something new and different—not to be part of the majority of people who are comfortable doing things in a familiar pattern. When I made the first laser in 1960, I found out firsthand how satisfying it can be to stay with an idea you believe in.

From the public relations standpoint, the press announcement of that laser was extraordinarily successful. The news hit the front page of every major newspaper in the United States and of many papers overseas. Unfortunately, a typical headline read: "LOS ANGELES MAN DISCOVERS SCIENCE FICTION DEATH RAY!"

Shortly thereafter, the owner of Knotts Berry Farm, a popular amusement park, phoned. He wanted to use the laser in a shoot-the-duck game. A representative of the Ice Capades wanted laser light for the spotlights on his performers because of its purity. The president of the American Meat Packers Association wanted to use a laser to stun hogs. Here were three forward-thinking, progressive, entrepreneurial people who looked on lasers as a tool they could use creatively in their work. Whether it was feasible or not was beside the point. They were ready to try.

Nearly forty years later, the laser is still as exciting and marvelous as it was in its "gee whiz!" days. I'm no longer pulled aside at scientific conferences and asked, "Do you think the laser is ever really going to be useful?" Instead, when someone reads my name badge, they may say, "My grandmother's eyesight was saved because of laser surgery," or even, "Thank you for my job."

The acceptance of lasers came rather slowly, just like that of the airplane and the auto. I seriously doubt that the Wright brothers ever dreamed there would be flights around the world and planes carrying hundreds of passengers. And for many years, automobiles were looked on as a rich man's toy. I certainly didn't envision lasers becoming part of everyday life . . . as familiar as the supermarket checkout scanner or the compact audio disc.

From the beginning, I thought lasers could be used in medicine, but I didn't dream how fantastic today's results would be or the difference they would make in diagnosis and surgery. I felt lasers would be used in communication, but I didn't really see how. It wasn't practical until low-loss fiber was invented ten years later.

Today, lasers in manufacturing improve yield and productivity. You can cut through half an inch of steel with a laser faster than just about any other way. Today, lasers are used for computer printers and extremely high-density information storage. And tomorrow, tiny lasers inside a computer will achieve much faster speed and performance with optical computing than digital computers now offer. It's even conceivable that lasers could be the key to solving the energy problem through laser fusion!

To me, lasers are one of the fastest growth industries in the world. There will be jobs in laser technology, not only in working with current laser applications, but also jobs that don't yet exist. The courage of young people—people who are not afraid to go ahead with ideas they believe in, despite possible discouragement—will make those jobs possible.

Books such as this, which help introduce young people to lasers, play an important role in stimulating imagination and creativity. I hope the laser brings as much satisfaction to your life as it has to mine.

Ted Maiman
Inventor of the first working laser

Editor's note: Physicist and inventor Theodore (Ted) Maiman died on May 5, 2007, after an extraordinary career. Several years earlier he had written this foreword and contributed an interview, information, and suggestions for the first edition of this book.

Acknowledgments

THE FOLLOWING INDIVIDUALS were especially helpful in the development of this book: Gary Benedict, Edesly Canto, Patrick Doolan, Ellet Drake, Jack Dyer, Robert Ford, Gordon Gould, Susan Hicks, Joe Hlubucek, Reena Jabamoni, Rick Jackson, Frank Jacoby, Tung H. Jeong, James Johnson, Alan J. Jones, Hamid Madjid, Fortunez Massuda, Vivian Merchant, George L. Paul, Jeri Peterson, Judith Pfister, Robert Prycz, Greg Rixon, Howard Rudzinsky, John Ruselowski, George Sanborn, Fred Seaman, M. J. Soileau, Doris Vila, and Carol Worth.

Special gratitude for the help of the late Theodore (Ted) H. Maiman, inventor of the laser, on the first edition of this book, and whose memory lives on in this new edition.

The author also acknowledges the assistance of the Accreditation Board for Engineering and Technology, Alberta Laser Centre, American Association of Engineering Societies, American Society for Laser Medicine and Surgery, Australian Embassy, Battelle Laboratories, Bell Labs, British Information Service, Edison Foundation, Electronic Engineering Associates, Gas Research Institute, Hewlett-Packard, Institute of Industrial Engineers, Lake Forest College, Laser Focus/Electro-Optics, Laser Institute of America, Lawrence Livermore National Laboratories, Optical Society of America, Raycon Corporation, School of the Art Institute of Chicago, Society of Manufacturing Engineers, Society of Women Engineers, SPIE, University of Arizona Optical Sciences Center, University of Central Florida/CREOL, University of Rochester Institute of Optics, and Westinghouse.

The author also wishes to thank Barbara Wood Donner for her help in revising the current edition.

1

LASER: A REVOLUTIONARY LIGHT

ON AN OTHERWISE ordinary day in May 2005, a message was sent—and received—between NASA's Goddard Space Center and the *Messenger* spacecraft, which was gently turning and moving on its path far out in space. This time the message was not a missive of words relayed from Earth to satellite to spacecraft, or microwaves sent to spread broadly outward into the firmament, but just a wink—a direct, eye-to-eye, laser-lit, celestial wink—that passed between the two of them, gleaming across fifteen million miles directly to its target for the very first time in history.

Two lasers, one aboard the *Messenger* and one at Goddard, continued to pulse back and forth for a time, while members of the NASA teams who had brought about this long-hoped-for and hard-won contact laughed and grinned and hugged each other, because it had finally, really, actually worked! That glorious fifteen-million-mile wink proved that Earth could communicate far out into space and would one day transmit complex messages back and forth between planets, space stations, space ships, and perhaps even solar systems and galaxies.

Ted Maiman's Vision

Nearly a half-century before, one man had imagined that it could be done this way—with laser light. As long ago as 1960, when physicist Ted Maiman had made his first red-ruby laser glow with an amplified light, he listed the ways he could envision the laser being used. He said then that he could see it lighting through space, outward to other planets, reaching much farther than any light humankind had ever made. Back then, not many people listened. There were other inventions to be developed—other accomplishments to be made that could be more clearly envisioned and turned into profit more quickly.

So it took a while before Ted Maiman's voice became heard above the others. But once the idea of his intense and glowing beam of light caught on, the reality of laser spread and gained momentum; one after another, scientists, inventors, and entrepreneurs took hold of it. From large laboratories to small job shops, to businesses, medical centers, vast communications companies, and the world's largest and most powerful universities and research centers, the laser grew into a global phenomenon.

Ted Maiman died on May 5, 2007, after decades of creative work and leadership in the field of laser research that his own invention had helped to begin. Having inspired thousands of students and scientists over the years, he was honored the world over. Nobel-winning physicist Charles H. Townes wrote of Ted Maiman in an obituary for the *New York Times*, "As creator of the first operating laser, he has left an enduring mark on science and technology."

Maiman's friends held a tribute on May 16, the forty-seventh anniversary of his invention.

In the span of his lifetime, Ted Maiman had seen his invention grow from the first glowing light that he could hold in his hands to the powerful beam that spanned fifteen million miles. In the time of our own lives, no matter our ages, we have seen laser technology gain momentum and become a scientific revolution.

The laser is as revolutionary to our use of light as the computer has been to our use of information. Both technologies have become available to us in relatively recent times, and each has opened the way to previously unimagined and breathtaking changes in the way that we do things, expanding immeasurably the power of what human technology can accomplish. Each has created a revolution in its area of human endeavor. Together they have opened vast new opportunities for healing the human body, producing useful goods and services, and communicating new knowledge and awareness—not only of ourselves and our planet, but of our solar system and of the universe beyond.

From Its Slow Beginning to the Speed of Light

Laser technology is growing very rapidly in all kinds of applications. Every day thousands of bright red or green beams flash from familiar handheld laser pointers. Thousands of factory welders use lasers that greatly speed their production. Hundreds of lasers are manufactured for military target detection. Thousands of nearsighted people walk into medical centers with fuzzy eyesight and receive the laser procedure called Lasek that allows them to walk out the same day with restored vision—many to discard their glasses or contact lenses for the first time in decades. And perhaps most common of all, millions of people are entertained and informed each day by laser-recorded sound and images on CDs and DVDs.

Laser technology has created thousands of new jobs for providing all these goods and services and many more. Because of lasers, thousands of patients receive faster and more accurate medical diagnostic tests, experience less pain in surgeries, are able to quit smoking more easily, or simply have unwanted body hair quickly removed—all because of the ubiquitous laser. Laser light is the basis of a marvelously useful and effective technology, and only a few decades ago, it was being called "the invention without a purpose."

The possibility of the laser was originally described by Albert Einstein in the early years of the twentieth century, but lasers were not developed for a half century more and were first introduced for general public use within the past couple of decades.

Once it got started, laser development blossomed at breathtaking speed; but at first it was somewhat slow to be understood, and introducing it to the public took work.

Introducing Laser Light to the Public

People had to be taught about the laser, and scientists who understood and used it were convinced that the public would respond. When laser expert M. J. Soileau visited fourth-grade classrooms more than two decades ago, he carried a very humble sort of laser with him. It was nothing like a modern, slim, lightweight pen laser but instead was just a small black cube about the size of a lunch box. Children were intrigued and crowded around him asking what it was.

When Soileau told them the black box was a laser, they often refused to believe him. To them, the word *laser* conjured up images of the lightstick used by Jedi warriors in *Star Wars* and certainly not something like this plain, ordinary-looking black box.

Soileau welcomed the children's skepticism. As head of the University of Central Florida's Center for Research and Education in Optics and Lasers (CREOL), he was accustomed to people not really understanding what lasers were, and he was eager to tell the children about them.

"Don't lasers make holes in things?" was usually one of their questions. Soileau explained that some lasers can indeed make holes and are used for that reason in many industrial and medical applications. However, many lasers are not powerful enough to do anything more than appear very bright. As director of the programs at CREOL, Soileau worked tirelessly to introduce the general public to the phenomenon of laser light.

Still Mysterious and Increasingly Powerful

Although most people still don't truly understand lasers, the phenomenon of laser light fascinates us all. When we think of lasers, we imagine powerful bursts of light—cool or with intense levels of heat—and highly advanced technology. Lasers can be all of that and more. Since the mid-twentieth century, lasers have been the catalysts for radical changes in industry, medicine, communications, and science. Without our even being aware of it, lasers have become the agents of change in hundreds of aspects of our daily lives.

What Is a Laser?

If you are not already a scientist, it may be difficult to imagine what a laser is. Picture someone shining a light into a closed box, making the light go through a medium—in some cases, a bright red ruby or a sapphire stimulated to emit more light—and then bouncing the light between a series of mirrors, until it is amplified into becoming a finely focused and linear beam, which is superbright. This is a very general and not very scientific description, but now let's take a look at a scientific one.

The word *laser* itself is an acronym for light amplification by stimulated emission of radiation. Radiation in this sense is another word for electromagnetic energy, which includes light.

A laser is a device that generates or amplifies coherent radiation at frequencies in the infrared, visible, or ultraviolet regions of the electromagnetic spectrum.

Laser light has several properties that make it different from regular light. First, it is *collimated*—meaning that it travels for long distances in a narrow beam rather than fragmenting off in many directions as regular light does.

Continuous beams or shorts bursts of laser light can be used to create different effects. Because it is focused narrowly, the light from a laser can be much more intense than regular light, especially in bursts. The power from a laser beam can be just a few microwatts, or it can be several billion watts or more in short bursts.

The *coherence* of laser light is another important factor. Laser light waves stay synchronized over long distances. And laser light is only one color, making it monochromatic. Some laser beams that produce light in the infrared or ultraviolet wavelengths are also invisible.

Many Uses of Lasers

Look up into the night sky over many a large city today, and you will see beams of almost impossibly bright and intense fuschia and gold and green laser light streaming from the tops of tall buildings. Look down into the decorative reflecting ponds at resort hotels and amusement parks, and watch lovely laser-light patterns and displays illuminating the water. Look out onto nighttime games at soccer and football fields, and you can see fast-moving halftime laser-light shows that are positively breathtaking.

In the world of lasers today, we know and appreciate that laser light is piercing the sky, used by astrophysicists in exploration and measurement of space. We move around bright little lasers beneath our hands when we move the computer mouse around on its mouse pad. We can hear the distinct quality of sound on the CDs and DVDs that we love best, and we can enjoy the intense and vivid color of the images and appreciate that the laser technology that supplies these particular applications was not even in existence just a few years ago.

With all the different kinds of laser light that are used in our everyday lives, the most familiar are those used to record, transmit, and store information.

Sound and Image Recording

When we listen to music or look at movies with CD or DVD players, we are utilizing the power of lasers. The sounds and images are recorded by a laser beam, which burns a pattern of dots onto a disc. Then a tiny semiconductor laser in our CD or DVD player reads those dots and converts them back into sound and images. Not only can the laser record faster and make more perfect copies, but the quality of the recording itself is many times more intense and pure.

Quality of sound recording took a great leap forward with the use of the CD, and it became even better with the use of DVD. Because only the light from the laser touches the disk, you hear a very clean and clear sound without the interference of scratches and dust that you would hear with an old-style tape or vinyl recording. Laser-recorded images are sharp and clear as well.

Information Recording

Just as DVD recorder/players have almost replaced other methods of sound and image recording, the process of laser recording and storing of information has revolutionized libraries and other warehouses of information. Lasers are used to create the DVDs and CDs that store databases, encyclopedias, art, and many other kinds of information that we regularly access by computer.

Scanning and Printing

After we have used a DVD or CD-ROM disc and found information that we need for a school or work report, for example, lasers are also involved when we print up that report on a laser printer. Laser printers print quickly, creating pages that look as if they were printed professionally. The scanning laser within the printer moves across a light-drum, which attracts ink where the laser has hit and transfers the ink to the paper as it is rolled across.

Scanning lasers are used to read as well as to write. Every time you buy groceries at a supermarket, tools at a hardware store, or clothing at a department store, a laser-powered scanner reads the labels with the Universal Product Code striped patterns and rings up the price.

Communication

Let's say you want to call some friends on a landline telephone. Fiber-optic cables that are used by most telephone companies employ tiny semiconductor lasers to carry your call across town or around the world. The sound of your voice is converted to electrical pulses and then converted to laser light that can travel through the fiber-optic cables. Using lasers to carry telephone calls is far more efficient than the earlier technology that sent calls over copper wires. Because lasers can pulse very rapidly, one miniscule glass fiber can transmit the calls of thousands of copper wires.

Manufacturing

The manufacturing industry uses lasers in factories to produce an astonishing array of products and materials. Lasers can be powerful enough to cut through thick pieces of strong metal such as steel and precise enough to drill two hundred holes on the head of a pin. Lasers also are used to weld metal, solder tiny circuits for electronics parts, drill miniscule holes, and cut cloth for clothing.

Measuring

Lasers provide an extremely accurate way of taking measurements. Using lasers, we are able to calculate distances on Earth and in space much more precisely than ever before. In 1969, astronauts placed a highly durable and shiny reflector on the moon that can reflect back a laser beam to its corresponding system here on Earth. With that reflection, scientists can calculate the distance accurately. Advanced laser installations have been built in every developed country to explore and measure distances and phenomena in space.

Military Uses

Globally, various military forces use lasers to aim "smart bombs" that can follow moving targets and even distinguish some types of targets from others. They use lasers in advanced technology to guide planes, explore features of unknown terrain, and detect and identify unknown forms of various kinds in the dark or in bad weather. Lasers of different kinds are also used to simulate the explosiveness of real ammunition for training exercises.

Medical and Cosmetic Uses

Many illnesses, injuries, and deformities are also being cured with the aid of lasers. Doctors in almost every specialty use lasers for a host of procedures, including repairing injured tissue, killing or removing cancerous growths, correcting vision problems, and even erasing spots and lines and wrinkles!

Entertainment and Marketing

Laser light shows can light up the sky and are used for special effects in movies, presentations, advertising commercials, and cartoons. They provide emphasis, entertainment, and fun at sports events, local and international competitions, celebrations of the completion of new buildings, political campaigns, enormous outdoor concerts, and state and county fairs.

From tiny lasers like the one in a handheld pointer to the world's biggest laser, which is housed at Lawrence Livermore National Laboratory in California, lasers have taken a prominent place in many aspects of our lives. Thousands of skilled technicians, technologists, researchers, and specialists are employed to carry out the work of laser technology.

It is hard to imagine that the first practical working laser was not even invented until 1960. Unlike most inventions, which are created to address a particular need or problem, lasers were developed before there were any specific applications for them. Since that time, scientists have developed and refined many different kinds of lasers to serve different needs; hundreds of educational and training courses have been established; and hundreds of companies, professional associations, licensing and certifying agencies, and laboratories and clinics have been created to train the people, manufacture the equipment, and provide the leadership and the services to deliver the benefits of laser technology to consumers worldwide.

The possibilities for laser use keep growing as new applications are continuously being developed, and the different kinds of opportunities to work with them are increasing as well. In this book you will find an introduction to this technology, to the major fields that it serves, and to the requirements and rewards of devoting a career to laser technology, as well as references to a breadth of resources for further information, as a student and as a professional.

Birth of a New Industry

From its humble beginning, laser science grew into a complex science—complexity and variety are characteristic of the intricate and burgeoning laser industry. Like the branches of a tree, the applications of laser technology have thrust outward in hundreds of different directions.

The inventor, Ted Maiman, calculated that the whole nine-month project that resulted in the first operating laser cost Hughes Aircraft only about $50,000 to complete, including his own salary, his assistant's salary, and overhead—a terrific bargain when you consider that the worldwide market today earns revenues of billions of dollars each year!

Included in this book are descriptions of some of the exciting opportunities available to people who want to work in this fast-growing field. Only a few years ago, lasers were so exotic that they were the exclusive domain of Ph.D.s and other advanced scientists. Now we encounter laser technology in cosmetics, health care, retailing, electronics, astrophysics, military applications, physics research, safety and traffic control, entertainment and advertising, and many more areas that we work with every day. Opportunities for a career in laser technology are virtually limitless.

Laser Patent War

Patent disputes are often fought for pride and prestige, although some are fought for money. With the first laser patents, there was no money to fight for, and only a few people thought that there might ever be any in the future.

Development of the laser was complicated by people not understanding its potential and by a number of challenges to its patents. The controversy over patent rights is one of the more fascinating aspects of the early years of the laser. The laser "patent war," which began in 1957 in the physics department at Columbia University, raged on for more than thirty years and caused many divisions and a great deal of expense within the laser world.

The battle was about who had first come up with the idea for the laser. Was it Dr. Charles H. Townes, a physics professor at Columbia, and Arthur L. Schawlow, his brother-in-law and research partner at Bell Laboratories? Or was it Gordon Gould, who was then a thirty-seven-year-old graduate student at Columbia?

The U.S. Patent Office has a procedure for deciding who has the right to a patent where claims overlap in applications—a situation the Patent Office calls "interference." Gould's patent application contained many inventions, including two different types of lasers, and it covered various other aspects of lasers. There were also five other interferences filed from other inventors.

Most important was one filed by the inventor Charles Townes. In 1951, while he was continuing experiments that were begun in Germany by others, he proposed separating a beam of ammonia molecules into two portions. The molecules in the two portions of the beam did not have the same energy states; one of the two energy states was higher. Early scientists studying the branch of physics known as quantum mechanics had believed previously that if an electromagnetic beam with a particular resonant frequency was passed through a medium, molecules of the beam in a higher state of energy might be stimulated to fall to a lower state of energy and in the process might reinforce the primary beam.

Townes used a microwave oscillator in his experiments. He passed the high-energy portion of his ammonia beam through a cavity that resonated at a frequency that matched the energy difference between the high- and low-energy states.

Eventually Townes was awarded a patent for his *maser*, a word coined as an acronym for microwave amplification by stimulated emission of radiation. Masers and lasers are theoretically similar, but masers operate at frequencies in the microwave region of the spectrum, while lasers operate in the light range of the spectrum. Later on, the Townes patent was licensed to laser manufacturers.

Meanwhile, at Bell Laboratories Arthur Schawlow was continuing research on optical masers. Working together, Schawlow and Townes proposed a new way to get optical maser action. Their plan was for an alkaline vapor to be placed in an optical cavity to serve as an active medium, which could be excited in such a way that if an optical wave were present, it would be amplified as it moved through the medium. According to Gould, Schawlow and Townes didn't realize the active medium could be excited by light.

The work of Townes and Schawlow acquired U.S. Patent Number 2,929,922 in 1960. Because they had applied for a patent before Gould's original application, they were considered the "senior parties."

Gould was unable to establish a date for his work that was earlier than their patent application. What the Schawlow and Townes patent claimed to cover, Gould said, was the resonator—a pair of mirrors required to shine the light back and forth through the laser amplifier.

In 1964, Townes was awarded the Nobel Prize in physics for developing the laser and maser, so it seemed that the issue had been settled. Gould, however, had not given up the fight to have his claims recognized by the U.S. Patent Office. It was a long and difficult struggle. The Patent Office eventually required Gould to divide his original application into six different applications.

Each challenge, or interference, to his patents took several years to resolve. Also, they were run in sequence, so the determination of the last one was not completed until 1973, fourteen years after Gould had originally filed. By that time, the industry had virtually forgotten there was such a thing as the Gould patent applications.

The laser industry had grown quite a lot by 1977, the year in which Gould was finally issued his first patent on amplifiers. By then there were many companies, many laser products, and many ways in which lasers were being used.

"The amount of money involved for royalties was big enough." Gould said, "that nobody was going to just write me a check if I called them up and told them about my patents."

Two of Gould's most important patents covered two different kinds of amplifiers that built up the strength of the light beam. One amplifier was the so-called *optically pumped laser*, consisting of a rod of appropriate material, such as ruby, with a flashlamp beside it. The light from the flashlamp excites the ruby to a state where it serves as an amplifier. Eventually, nearly a third of all lasers were optically pumped—making that patent a significant one.

Gould's second patent, issued in 1979, covered laser use for several processes: welding, heat treating, evaporating materials, and similar reactions that require heat.

The third Gould patent, issued in 1987, was probably the most important of all. It covered a different kind of amplifier, the *discharge laser*. When this patent was issued, U.S. Senator Arlen Spector of Pennsylvania held an award ceremony to honor Gould. Because Senator Spector headed the subcommittee that oversaw the U.S. Patent Office, his recognition of Gould's work was important. In that year, after many hearings and contradictory claims, fully three decades after the controversy had begun, Gould won an important victory when he was awarded the patent that covered gas discharge lasers.

Gould received another laser patent in 1988—the "Brewster angle window patent." Some laser tubes have slanted windows on the end. When they are at a particular angle (Brewster's angle), laser gas can pass through them without any loss of power.

After his years of applying for patents and dealing with the interference patents filed by others, Gould had learned a great deal about how the patent system works. He commented that, "The awarding of patents was established in the U.S. Constitution. Our forefathers felt there should be a patent system to give an inventor some rights to his invention . . . to encourage inventors to get the inventions out. . . . Yet it's clear that if it takes twenty-eight years to get a patent issued, the system is not working as intended."

He advised other inventors to apply for patents for all aspects of their inventions and said, "The more patents you have, the less likely it is that someone will attempt to overturn them."

Importance of the Gould Patents

The question of patent rights was important for many reasons, especially financial ones. Whoever held the patent rights stood to receive potentially very large royalties for the use of their inventions in the developing laser industries. Gould, of course, contended for nearly thirty years that he should be recognized and awarded the patents for his work.

With patents in hand and a strong determination to win what he felt was due him, Gould sued various laser companies, charging that they had infringed on his patent rights. These were not easy legal battles. A court victory in 1987 against one of the leading laser companies was pivotal because it established that Gould's patents were valid.

Millions of dollars were at stake, including penalties for infringement and royalties that involved more than two hundred laser manufacturers—royalties that Gould expected would rise to $20 million per year. As a result of winning the pivotal suit, Patlex Corporation, which owned a 64 percent interest in the Gould patent, began licensing companies to use the laser patented by Gould.

Gould patents covered optically pumped discharge-excited laser amplifiers, which eventually were used in approximately 80 percent of industrial, commercial, and medical applications, and revenue from the patents reached into the millions of dollars.

Opportunities in laser technology—the numbers and variety of the jobs that you may hope to hold—are related to the financial health of the companies and other organizations involved with lasers, a health that may hinge on their financial obligations with respect to the Gould patents. The years ahead will continue to be influenced by the financial costs of these obligations.

2

How Lasers Work

WHETHER A LASER is used to entertain a massive outdoor crowd at a famous performer's concert or to perform delicate surgery on a patient's eye, it is operating on the same principle. Light amplification by stimulated emission of radiation, or *laser*, indicates a device that generates or amplifies emitted light.

This description encompasses many different kinds of lasers. Some lasers are solid-state. Others use gases, such as helium and neon (He-Ne), argon, krypton, or carbon dioxide. Ion lasers are used in the printing industry, in light shows, and in therapeutic and diagnostic medicine. Diode (or semiconductor) lasers have proven to be valuable in such uses as optical disks and for communications.

According to a 2007 report by *Laser Focus World*, the worldwide market for diode lasers reached $3.1 billion in 2006. Revenues were slightly down from 2005 totals, but unit numbers increased, primarily due to continued growth in use of diode lasers in telecommunications and high-power diode applications.

As more individuals and organizations turn to the Internet, the increased need for fiber-optic networks is expected to increase the demand for diode lasers. Other laser devices, including dye lasers and excimer lasers, are also expected to increase in use.

Parts of a Laser

Although there are many types of lasers in use today, it is still true that, in general, a laser is made up of four parts:

1. An active medium made up of atoms, molecules, ions, or a semiconducting crystal
2. A mechanism that excites the atoms, molecules, ions, or semi-conducting crystal into higher energy levels than their normal state
3. Elements that let radiation bounce back and forth many times through the active medium, amplifying the light
4. An output coupler—a special mirror at one end of the laser that is constructed so that some of the laser light can be allowed to escape from the active medium, resulting in a highly controlled and focused beam

One argument used unsuccessfully in a lawsuit over the Gould patent was that laser light occurs in nature. The laser manufacturer suggested that sunlight stimulating the atmosphere of the planet Mars was causing a lasing action. The Martian surface acted as a highly reflective mirror, and the interface between space and the Martian atmosphere acted as an output mirror. Since the components common to all lasers (an energy source, something being lased, and two mirrors) exist as a natural phenomenon, the manufacturer said, lasers should not be patentable.

The courts did not, however, buy this argument and continued to uphold the validity of the Gould patents, recognizing that it was not so much the medium being used as it was the process of stimulating and directing the light that was at issue.

"Just about anything can be stimulated," commented Gary Benedict, then chairman of the Laser Council of the Society of Manufacturing Engineers. "The Americans have made a laser out of Jell-O, and the Russians, out of vodka."

How Lasers Amplify Light

Ruby and sapphire have been among the many different kinds of media that have been used in the manufacture of lasers. The purpose of the excitation mechanism, however, remains the same—to excite the electrons or ions that the medium contains, regardless of what active medium is used.

Scientists think of electrons as traveling around the nucleus of an atom in various orbits. When an electron is excited, the electron jumps to an orbit with a higher energy level. When it returns to the ground state, it gives off energy in the form of a tiny bundle of electromagnetic energy called a *photon*. If the photon comes near another electron from a different atom—an electron that is in this persistent higher energy state—the photon can induce the premature transition of the second electron so that it, too, gives off a photon.

Dr. Hamid Madjid, associate professor of physics at Pennsylvania State University, gave the following explanation:

> One photon stimulates the in-step emission of the second photon. Each of these two photons can pass another electron and release it, so pretty soon you have four photons, and eight photons, and

sixteen photons, and so forth, and you start generating coherent photons.

This occurs either in a glass tube filled with a mixture of gases, or in a solid material, such as a ruby rod. If those coherent photons move in the axis of the tube or the rod, they induce stimulated emission of more photons.

On one side of the laser there is a reflecting mirror; on the other, a semitransparent mirror that lets a little light through. The reflecting mirror bounces the small amount of laser light back into the active medium, where it is amplified again and again. This mirror is a special mirror that reflects almost all of the laser light that strikes it. The second mirror, called the output coupler, lets much of the light reflect back into the tube but also lets some of the amplified light escape. This amplified light is called the laser beam.

Race to Create the Laser

In 1959, research papers about laser light were available, and it was reported that a ruby crystal was not very efficient as a medium. A young research scientist at Hughes Aircraft Company in Malibu, California, decided to test for himself whether a ruby crystal was really as inefficient as was said. His name was Ted Maiman.

Maser and Laser

The maser already existed. Would it be possible to produce something similar, using optical instead of microwave frequencies, to stimulate the emission of radiation and amplify the light?

"The race was on," Ted Maiman recalled years later. "Universities and major research labs wanted to be first to make a laser." Among the players were Bell Telephone Labs; the Radiation Laboratory at Columbia University; the RCA Labs in Princeton, New

Jersey; the Schenectady Research Lab of General Electric; the IBM Labs; and the Lincoln Laboratory of MIT. Meanwhile, other researchers were hard at work in Great Britain, Germany, Japan, and other countries.

Looking for a Better Way

Although all of the scientists were working hard to be first, Maiman had an especially suited background that may have been responsible for his success in making the first working laser. He had earned his Ph.D. in physics and was an experimental physicist. He knew the theory and concepts of lasers, and he had practical lab experience with a background in electronics—along with intense motivation and drive. Maiman's Ph.D. dissertation, completed four years earlier, had included work in microwaves and optics. He knew about masers and had worked with them, but he believed they would not prove to be practical, because the maser required cooling to within a few degrees of absolute zero. Generating "coherent" light by the concept of stimulated emission sounded more feasible to him.

Power of Coherent Light

Coherence is one of the unique properties of laser light that makes it so valuable and so important in many laser applications. Coherence can be thought of as an *ordered phenomenon.*

Light from an incandescent bulb, such as an electric light, is incoherent. The light waves coming from that bulb differ from each other in frequency and wavelength, direction, and phase. These are difficult concepts to understand unless you have studied physics. We'll examine them, one at a time.

Light Waves

Scientists believe that light travels in waves, like waves on the ocean. Each wave has a high point, called a *peak* or *crest*, and a low point, called a *trough*. If you were standing on a platform in the ocean, holding your hand out horizontally, as each wave passed by, the crest of the wave would touch your hand. The number of times that happened—that is, how many crests went by in each second—is called *frequency*. Frequency is measured in units of reciprocal time—for example, one per second.

Frequency Coherence

Ordinary light coming from an incandescent bulb or even from the sun is jumbled up. Its light waves vary in frequency. In contrast, all the waves of laser light are identical—or coherent—in frequency, since they originate from identical atomic transitions. The word used to describe frequency coherence is *monochromaticity*.

Electromagnetic Spectrum

Scientists have discovered there is an electromagnetic spectrum of varying kinds of energy. The oscillations and waves within this spectrum produce both electrical and magnetic effects. Most of these energies are invisible. We can measure these waves, characterizing them by frequency and wavelength. For convenience, we divide the electromagnetic spectrum into sections. These sections are classified by the ways in which these energies are generated and used. The electromagnetic waves that have the lowest frequencies are *radio waves*. Next are *microwaves*. Above the microwaves (but still invisible to us) are *infrared* frequencies. We can feel these frequencies as heat, even though we do not see them.

Visible light is an extremely narrow part of the electromagnetic spectrum. The colors that we know, and can see, range from red, starting at a wavelength of 760 nanometers, to violet, which ends at a wavelength of 360 nanometers. (A nanometer is equal to one-billionth of a meter.) Above visible light on the electromagnetic spectrum come *ultraviolet light, x-rays,* and *gamma rays.*

Light and Color

The "white" light from an incandescent bulb or the sunlight that we see is really made up of many different colors. You can prove this yourself by looking at a beam of light before and after it is passed through a prism. The prism breaks the light up into its different colors.

Laser light contains light that is virtually of only one color. This color can vary, of course. In fact, lasers can produce frequencies and wavelengths that range from those of infrared rays through visible light and into ultraviolet light. The light from any one laser is concentrated into an extremely narrow band of frequencies. A laser's beam might be red, yellow, green, or blue, but it will be monochromatic—that is, of only one color.

Spatial Coherency

Direction and phase are also important concepts. Imagine a group of people who do not know each other walking across a bridge. They are not all moving in step. Some go one way, while others go another. Some people are a little ahead; others lag behind. Ordinary light has wave patterns like this group of people. It is called *spatially incoherent.* The waves do not come at regular intervals. They are not all moving in the same direction.

Laser light is different—it has *spatial coherency*. Waves of laser light are somewhat like a large, well-disciplined marching band crossing a bridge—each row marching exactly the same distance from the row in front and the row in back. Because the band members are all marching in step, every one of those hundreds of people puts her or his foot down at the same time, generating far more force upon the bridge and in the airwaves than random walkers would. You can imagine how their combined steps make the bridge tremble and the noise resound. Laser light works in the same way. Because it is spatially coherent, the electric field reaches a maximum for all the little wavelengths that are acting in unison, all at the same time. The coherence of laser light greatly multiplies its strength and power.

Breakthrough Laser

By 1960, when Ted Maiman was a young Hughes corporation researcher, scientists were already used to working with coherent light from radiation. Ordinary radio waves, the AM radio, the FM radio, VHF (where television is on the electromagnetic spectrum), UHF (the higher bands of television), and even microwaves were already being used in different applications. If coherent light could actually be generated, it would be an important breakthrough, because light waves are about ten thousand times higher in frequency than the microwave section of the spectrum.

Maiman was eager to try. He considered using potassium vapor, an idea Townes and Schawlow had suggested. He considered using an electrical discharge similar to that in a neon sign—an idea that other researchers had proposed. What he really wanted, however, was a simple, rugged, solid material—one that was fluorescent, so its crystals would glow under ultraviolet light. Since he was already familiar with the optical properties of the synthetic ruby crystal from his earlier work with masers, Maiman turned to the ruby and decided to experiment with it.

The problem that had been identified with using the ruby, however, was that ruby light might not be strong enough. One of the earlier research papers reported that if you stimulated the ruby by shining ordinary (incoherent), ultraviolet, green, or blue light on it, the ruby would glow red. But the efficiency of that fluorescence was extremely low, and only 1 percent of the energy would be released in the glow. The remaining energy would be absorbed in the ruby.

Maiman returned to the ruby, trying to understand why the fluorescent process was as inefficient as the paper reported. There were a number of reasons why this could happen, and he looked at all of them, measuring carefully. To his surprise, when he had completed his work he discovered that the predicted inefficiency was incorrect. He found that, instead of only 1 percent of the green "exciting" light being converted to the red light of the fluorescing ruby, more like 70 percent could be converted. Ruby became a real possibility as a medium.

Not everyone agreed with Maiman. Schawlow, working at Bell Labs, said his group had evaluated the ruby and concluded it was impossible to make it work as a laser. Maiman still believed strongly in his findings, even though he was competing with world-class scientists.

Maiman's supervisors at Hughes questioned the value of his project. They suggested that he switch to research on the developing technology of computers, but Maiman wanted to keep going. Reluctantly, they allowed him to continue his work.

By all Maiman's mathematical calculations, his device should work. His ruby crystal rod was ⅜ inches in diameter and ¾ inches long. The ends of the ruby cylinder were flat, parallel, and highly polished. He made the ends of the rod reflective by giving them a thin coating of silver. He carved away a small hole in the coating to allow the laser light to escape.

The crystal needed an outside energy source of extremely high intensity to excite the electrons. Maiman researched the characteristics of all known laboratory high-intensity lamps. He considered and then discarded the idea of using a mercury arc lamp, and finally he decided to look at electronic flash. "I went through every catalog of every manufacturer," Maiman said. "I found three lamps listed. They were different sizes but all had approximately the same intensity. To be on the safe side, I sent for samples of all three; but since it was the energy per unit area that counted, I chose the smallest one to try first.

"Usually a lamp like this is mounted in a glass envelope, and its base fits into a socket. I cut off the glass and took off the socket, so I had the bare spiral flashlamp. I mounted the ruby inside the spiral. Around the spiral, I put a very highly polished aluminum reflector. The total housing was just a little smaller than a man's fist."

Maiman theorized that when he turned on the flashlamp, the strobe would put out an extremely intense burst of energy. The ruby crystal, he thought, would absorb that light. The ions would fluoresce and give off red photons. If he could get enough intensity, the red photons would not only glow but also be amplified.

He predicted that it would take a very short time for light to travel along the length of the crystal and that the amplified light would start to leak out through the small hole he had made in the silver coating. Maiman set up a measuring apparatus, so he'd be able to confirm that he had in fact generated coherent light. Finally, there were no more problems to check out.

Maiman remembered the excitement and satisfaction of his moment of triumph: "I turned it on, and it worked—the first time! When the laser started to 'go,' at first the fluorescence was at the low excitation rate. But as we got the excitation higher and higher, the crystal began to act as an amplifier. Then the photons that happened to be going along the axis of the cylindrical rod hit the mirror at one end and were reflected exactly back on themselves to the other mirror!"

Importance of Maiman's Work

Maiman's achievement in building the first actual working laser was significant enough for him to be named to the National Inventors Hall of Fame. Yet, even though he had an actual working laser—the first ever built—it was hard to sell his supervisors at Hughes and other scientists on the importance of his success and what it might mean.

Initially the response was very disappointing. The first scientific publication to which he submitted his report actually turned it down. Finally, the British journal *Nature* published Maiman's results. A few weeks before the article appeared, the Hughes corporation flew Maiman to New York for a press conference to announce the working laser.

"That was my first encounter with media," Maiman was to recall. "I described how I thought lasers could be used in medicine and biology, in industry for cutting and welding, and in communications because of the information capacity and enormous possible bandwidth. One reporter asked, 'Is it going to be a weapon?'

"I told him I thought, as a practical application of lasers, a weapon is a far-fetched idea. The next day, major headlines in the *Los Angeles Herald* said I'd discovered a science fiction death ray!"

Ironically, the Hughes Corporation lost the foreign rights to the laser patents because the company did not file quickly enough. In 1967, after he found that Hughes wasn't processing the patents efficiently, Maiman left the corporation and formed his own company to manufacture lasers. The Patent Office, in accordance with its traditional adversarial view, challenged Maiman by saying that, since the ruby laser was "obvious," he should not be entitled to a patent for making one. Members of the Patent Office cited previously published papers by other scientists that they said proved their point.

Maiman countered by stating that the other scientists had all rejected the ruby medium and said that it would not work. At that critical point, Maiman gave the Hughes Corporation the chance to use his affidavit or to relinquish their claim and let him file for the patent. Executives at Hughes were delighted to proceed, and the patent was issued to the Hughes Corporation within two weeks.

It had taken several years for the trade experts to be convinced that lasers actually had value. That taught Maiman another valuable lesson—one that is worth passing on to others.

"If you have any idea you want to pursue, if you've really studied it and thought about it, despite the negative consensus by experts, then go for it! I still remember a class that one scientist was to give at a university in the summer of 1960, a class he canceled after my press conference on lasers. One of his announced topics was 'Why a Laser Cannot Work.'"

As research and development of the laser grew more and more rapidly over the years, Ted Maiman stood out in his dedication and leadership for the rest of his life. He became an honored, admired, and beloved figure in the laser industry. Through his scientific discipline, teaching, and leadership, he influenced thousands of professionals and students during a scientific career that spanned more than half a century. By the time of his death in 2007, lasers of many kinds were being used for previously unimagined feats of science, medicine, industry, and entertainment in countries all over the world.

3

LASERS IN HEALTH CARE
AND MEDICINE

MEDICAL LASERS REPRESENT an extremely fast-growing segment of the laser industry, and according to the April 2006 edition of the *Medical Laser Report*, the sales of the top twenty medical laser manufacturers had nearly doubled since 2002. Those top twenty manufacturers alone had almost $2 billion in sales, and growth for 2006 was expected to be even greater at approximately 21 percent. Much of this growth was in the aesthetic area, with plastic and cosmetic surgery and dental uses making strong gains.

One of the earliest uses of laser light was in health care. Workable lasers had barely been invented when scientists began to apply them to medicine. Some of the most important applications of laser technology are in the areas of major medical surgery, cosmetic and plastic surgery, dentistry, and ophthalmology.

As early as the first half of the 1960s, lasers were used to treat skin discoloration and to repair detached retinas. By the year 2000, laser surgery had become a well-established course of treatment and was being used for many kinds of illnesses. Today, the medical uses of lasers have developed into a worldwide industry worth billions of dollars each year.

Variety of Laser Applications

Lasers are used by medical specialists for everything from eliminating snoring to treating such life-threatening illnesses as cancer. They are used intensively in procedures involving the eye, helping to correct astigmatisms and treat disease and injuries. Having laser surgery performed on one's eyes is no longer considered either particularly risky or even unusual.

Because lasers have now been integrated into so many aspects of medicine, it is hard to say precisely how much money is spent each year on laser surgery and treatments. The medical laser equipment market, a good barometer of the growth of laser medicine, was worth billions of dollars in 2006, with the top-three producing nations being the United States, Japan, and China, in that order.

Quanta Technologies cites the April 2006 edition of *Medical Laser Report*, saying that the top twenty medical laser manufacturers have seen nearly a doubling of their revenues since 2002, approaching $2 billion.

Aesthetic Applications

The field of cosmetic medicine, one of the earliest growing markets for laser procedures, witnessed steady growth until about 2005, when the rate began to decline slightly. Part of the reason for the earlier steady growth was that the baby boom generation is getting older, and many of those seventy million boomers want cosmetic medicine to provide cures for the symptoms of aging.

Revenues for cosmetic laser procedures—including removing wrinkles, birthmarks, hair, scars, and tattoos—are still very good, but the effects of a declining economy may have an effect on this market in the United States, due to decline in consumers' discretionary spending.

Research and Pioneering Applications in Medicine

Scientific research into the possibilities of lasers in medicine remains strong worldwide. At large research institutes such as the Laser Center at Massachusetts General Hospital, medical researchers are working in a wide array of specialties, including cardiology, gynecology, neurosurgery, orthopedics, otolaryngology, and urology. At many medical research centers, such as the University of Oklahoma School of Medicine, interdisciplinary teams of biologists, biochemists, physicists, medical doctors, and specialists in a wide array of medical technologies work together in coordinated efforts to produce new techniques and bring them to the end-users and the consumer patients as quickly as possible.

Researchers at Emory University's Eye Center are using diode lasers to destroy abnormal eye tissue that leads to blindness in babies. And at Loyola University Oral Health Center, oral surgeons are applying laser technology with a device that looks like a ballpoint pen to perform biopsies and remove abnormalities from the mouth. These kinds of procedures may sound like science fiction or medical practices from a far-distant future, but they are simply a sign of how advanced the use of lasers in modern medicine has become. In fact, says a representative of the American Society for

Laser Medicine and Surgery (ASLMS), "in some medical specialties, virtually no practitioner works without a laser at hand."

The high intensity of laser light and the fact that it can be precisely focused allow physicians to control extremely delicate cutting and cauterizing of living tissues. "You can make a precise cut with very little damage to surrounding tissue," explained Dr. Ellet Drake, former executive director of ASLMS.

Reducing the Risk of Infection

One clear advantage of lasers is that they can be used without coming into contact with the surrounding region of the body being treated, so that there is almost no risk of infection. In addition, because the laser coagulates (seals off) blood vessels that it cuts, the surgical site is almost bloodless, giving the doctor a clear view.

Greater Accuracy and Safety

Because thermal lasers work primarily through heating and cauterizing tissue, the intensely focused laser beam can burn a minuscule hole with great accuracy. In some cases, a series of these tiny holes are burned into the area surrounding a lesion, helping to seal it off, further reducing risks of bleeding, spread of infection, and trauma to surrounding tissue.

Lasers Used in Medicine

In health care, several kinds of lasers are used, including the argon laser, the CO_2 laser, and the neodymium-doped yttrium aluminum garnet (Nd:YAG), often referred to as the *YAG*. The laser used for a particular medical procedure may depend primarily on where the wavelength of that laser is best absorbed. For example, the argon laser is effectively absorbed by tissues containing high concentrations of hemoglobin or melanin.

The carbon dioxide (CO_2) laser has a longer wavelength. James Johnson, consultant in safety and laser applications and author of two books on lasers, pointed out that any tissue that contains water will absorb the CO_2's wavelength. Consequently, the carbon dioxide laser is extremely useful for certain types of surgery because it can vaporize tissue. The CO_2 laser is used to treat certain types of cancers.

The YAG laser can be used with fiber-optic technology. Optical fibers are extremely thin threads of glass that can transmit light over a great distance with very little loss of intensity. Rays of laser light traveling down such fibers are reflected off the sides.

In certain medical procedures, called *endoscopies*, the flexible fiber-optic device is used to let doctors look directly into portions of the body that they otherwise could not see, such as the esophagus or lungs. Endoscopic examinations also allow doctors to treat certain conditions directly.

The YAG laser beam can pass through a flexible scope and down to the area needing treatment. The surgeon can direct the laser beam to the target and use the beam to cut out tumors. "The YAG laser penetrates tissue very deeply," Johnson explained, "but its energy is dissipated because it scatters over a large volume of tissue; consequently it's good for cauterizing."

In photodynamic therapy a tunable—that is, an adjustable—dye laser is used. Doctors can aim the laser beam at tissue that has been treated with special chemicals. Laser surgery then selectively kills the cancer cells.

In one investigational procedure that used the argon dye laser technique, a special drug—dihematoporphyrin ether (DHE)—was injected into cancer patients with large tumors that interfered with eating and swallowing. The drug was taken up only by the cancer cells.

Light emitted by the tunable argon dye laser is sent down the long, thin, hollow tube, or endoscope, to the portion of the esophagus where the cancer cells are located. Because DHE is a photoactive drug, it reacts when exposed to light of a particular color—in this case, the wavelength of the argon dye laser. The drug causes the cancer cells to disintegrate when the pulses of laser light hit them. Because the energy of electrons coming into the laser can be tuned, the resulting laser beam will be just the right wavelength to trigger the process and destroy the cancer cells by stimulating the desired chemical change.

Before this laser procedure was developed, patients probably would have been treated with a different sort of laser in a procedure that can damage healthy unshielded cells in the esophagus as well as the cancer cells. The argon dye laser technique, therefore, is much more selective and causes less tissue damage.

Dr. Stephen K. Heier at New York Medical College in Valhalla, New York, investigated this technique and found that the drug-and-laser treatment worked successfully to reopen the esophagus to near-normal or normal size. The patients found the procedure to be painless, and nearby normal tissue exposed to the laser light received only minimal damage from the procedure.

Extensive and ongoing research is also being conducted on many other kinds of lasers for health care, which will affect our health and also our opportunities for jobs and careers in this field.

Lasers in Ophthalmology

LASIK is a familiar term to most of us, and it stands for Laser-Assisted In-Situ Keratomileusis. This procedure, widely practiced in the United States and elsewhere, uses lasers to change the shape of structures in the eye, thereby correcting nearsightedness and some other conditions and greatly improving the patient's eyesight.

Soon after workable lasers had been invented, doctors and scientists began experiments to see if the technology could be used to treat eye disorders. By 1961 a group headed by Dr. Charles Campbell at Columbia Presbyterian Hospital in New York City became the first to use the laser to treat a detached retina. Several years later, Dr. Hugh Beckman used a laser to open tiny holes in the iris. This treatment, performed at Detroit's Sinai Hospital, demonstrated that lasers could be used successfully as a surgical instrument, as well as an aid to coagulation.

Because lasers give ophthalmologists an enormous amount of precision and control, there are dozens of uses for lasers in eye surgery. Lasers are frequently used to treat retinal tears and detachments, diabetic retinopathy, and glaucoma. They are also used for resurfacing (plastic surgery), refractive surgery, and after-cataract surgery.

The argon ion laser, which uses a medium of electrically charged argon gas for generating laser light, has been used extensively in eye treatment for a special reason. The argon ion laser gives off a blue-green light, a color that's strongly absorbed by red objects such as blood, so this laser provides a useful tool in coagulation.

Diabetic retinopathy is a common complication of diabetes in which abnormal blood vessels develop in the retina. With the argon ion laser, the ophthalmologist can release thousands of laser bursts that strike the retina in a predetermined pattern. These short bursts of light can slow or stop bleeding from the blood vessels.

Argon ion lasers also are used to treat macular degeneration—an eye condition that often develops when a person becomes old. The macula is the central portion of the retina. If it becomes diseased, fluids can leak out from behind it and hamper vision. The coagulating laser is used to help reduce the leaking.

Another form of glaucoma in which pressure buildup cannot be traced to a specific abnormality is also treated with laser. The ophthalmologist uses the laser to make a series of openings in the tissues that normally let fluid flow out from the front chamber of the eye.

Ophthalmologists also use a krypton laser, which is similar in design to the argon laser. It uses krypton, another gas. Ophthalmologists choose these lasers because of their photocoagulation abilities. Although the argon ion and krypton lasers produce an extremely small amount of heat, that heat can be delivered very precisely to the area the beam hits.

The YAG laser provides another option. Ophthalmologists like Dr. George Sanborn at Southwestern Medical School, University of Texas Health Science Center, Dallas, have used the Nd:YAG laser to treat certain types of glaucoma. They have also used it to treat a condition in which patients, who have had previous cataract surgery and had an artificial lens implanted, develop clouding in a normally clear membrane behind the lens.

"The YAG laser does not use heat," Sanborn explained. Rapid pulses of the Nd:YAG laser eliminate much of the clouded area of the membrane, yet they leave enough of it intact to hold the artificial lens implant in place.

Still another type of laser, the excimer laser, is being used—more often in Europe than in America—in a procedure that is called *radial keratotomy.*

"Ophthalmologists today regard many types of laser surgery as almost routine and not at all unusual," Sanborn said. "Today, most ophthalmologists receive training in laser surgery as part of their residency.

Lasers in Obstetrics/Gynecology

Reproductive endocrinologists like Dr. Reena Jabamoni, a fertility specialist, have been using lasers to help treat conditions that can interfere with conception. She has used the CO_2 laser for pelvic endometriosis, for reconstruction of fallopian tubes that have been damaged by endometriosis or pelvic inflammatory disease, and for removal of fibroids, which are benign tumors of the uterus. The endoscopic Nd:YAG laser can be used to treat excessive menstrual bleeding that is not caused by an underlying disease.

The CO_2 laser is used in gynecology because abnormal tissue can be vaporized or removed easily. It is used to remove lesions of the cervix, vulva, and vagina. Since much of a woman's reproductive system is accessible from outside the body, doctors also can use the CO_2 laser to remove a tiny cone-shaped section of the cervix for diagnosis. Such *laser conization* can be performed quickly and with little or no loss of blood.

Lasers also are used by gynecologists to treat other conditions. Genital warts, caused by a virus, can be removed with laser, and the recurrence rate is substantially less than with other forms of treatment. A laser inserted through a small incision in the abdomen can be used to treat adhesions of the ovary—a condition that affects fertility and occurs when the outside of the colon or another structure in the abdomen becomes attached to the surface of an ovary.

Lasers are also used by gynecologists for reconstructive surgery of the uterus. In a rare condition in which a woman has a uterus divided into two compartments, the gynecologist can use the laser to remove tissue from between the compartments, enlarging the uterus to one full-sized cavity that can hold a baby.

Procedures like laser laparoscopy are often performed as outpatient ambulatory surgery, and patients stay in the hospital for more extensive reconstructive laser surgery.

Most medical schools routinely instruct new residents in surgery and other specialties in the use of lasers, but other doctors who are already in practice acquire these skills in a variety of ways. Medical schools, hospitals, equipment manufacturers, and professional organizations offer a variety of courses and on-the-job training.

In one sequence, doctors take classes, then have hands-on experience in a laboratory—first with inanimate objects and then with animal experiments. Next, they work with a preceptor—someone who has very good training. After the preceptorship, the doctor will probably do a number of cases in a hospital setting, under the supervision of an experienced laser surgeon. One doctor commented, "Although the laser is precise, when you aim the beam, you are destroying tissue, layer by layer. Because you are working close to important organs such as the bladder, ureter, and bowel in vital areas of the body, you must be extremely controlled in your technique."

Keeping up with new developments in laser use is mandatory, and professional associations like the Gynecologic Surgery Society (GSS) and the American Society of Laser Medicine and Surgery (ASLMS), as well as others, are key participants in the continuing education of doctors in practice.

Lasers in Podiatry

Podiatrists are using lasers more and more in their practices. Just how much more, though, depends on the type of practice the doctor has. One doctor estimated that only 5 percent of her work involves laser surgery. "That's because I see a lot of patients with bunions and hammer toes," she explained. "I don't use lasers for bone surgery."

Laser surgery is useful for soft tissue conditions such as warts, plugged sweat glands, ingrown toe nails, and corns that are not due to a bone deformity. Laser surgery for these problems can be simple, quick, and relatively painless compared to conventional surgery. Many patients are less worried about surgery if it is to be done with a laser, expecting it to be easier and safer than conventional surgery.

From the patient's point of view, laser surgery is not difficult or prolonged. An associate or technician anesthetizes the area, and the surgeon uses the laser to cut out the diseased tissue and also to coagulate blood vessels. Often the surgeon can complete the surgery quite quickly. For instance, it is not unusual for the podiatrist to be able to remove a single wart in just a few minutes or a small group of warts in less than ten minutes. The associate then dresses the wound. After a brief rest and a period for questions and for instruction in caring for the wound, the patient is ready to leave the office in a relatively short time.

One important precaution is safety glasses. The doctor, patient, and anyone else in the room will wear them during some types of laser surgery because of the intensity and penetration power of the laser beam. The laser equipment vendors want to be sure that the doctors, technicians, nurse assistants, and laser coordinators are using the laser properly and safely, and they provide extensive user and safety training and in some cases a certification, for users. Vendors also usually continue to provide extensive seminars for use of new equipment, as technology advances and new products are developed.

Laser manufacturing companies often donate lasers to podiatry schools, so students can be trained in laser surgery. "It's good business for the companies," one doctor mentioned. "In addition to goodwill, they know that students who have done this surgery as part of their podiatric training will be comfortable when they use the laser."

Working with Lasers

Not everyone who works with lasers in health care is a physician, of course. Dental assistants and hygienists will assist with laser surgeries and treatments, which can save patients much of the pain, bleeding, and infection risks of conventional surgery. Laser nurses play an important role in hospital or clinic care. Sometimes these nurses also are designated as laser safety officers; at other times, a laser safety officer serves only in that post and does not function as a nurse. Nurse assistants, technicians, and others may assist with laser procedures in various medical treatment settings.

Laser Nurse Coordinator in a Hospital Setting

At one hospital-affiliated laser center in a major urban area, Robert served as laser nurse coordinator and as laser safety officer. A graduate of Northeastern Illinois University in secondary education and U.S. history, he spent ten years teaching mathematics in the public schools before deciding to make a career switch. Although he enjoyed teaching and wanted to work with people, he didn't like being transferred to a new school every few years, and he had found himself spending more and more time on paperwork.

In checking newspaper want ads to see where jobs were available, Robert found only a few possibilities for teachers, but more than ten times as many for nurses. Other family members who were nurses liked their careers and talked about the field often; Robert thought he, too, would enjoy nursing.

He enrolled in a hospital's school of nursing and graduated in two years. Because he had had a number of science courses in his undergraduate studies, he could shorten the study time usually required for the nursing curriculum. He passed the state examinations and became licensed as a registered nurse.

After working for a year in a rehabilitation unit, Robert saw an opening posted for a laser nurse. He interviewed with the hospital's medical director and was offered the position. Initially the hospital sent him to an intensive three-day workshop; after that, Robert said, it was basically on-the-job training, learning as much as he could from the physicians and by being around lasers. Today, certification is required, and laser nurses, coordinators, and others take more extensive courses to complete the certification.

A major hospital will usually use lasers in research, dermatology, general surgery, and gastroenterology, as well as eye procedures and other medical specialties. Laser nurse coordinators will divide their time between the laser center and the regular operating room.

Patients who can have laser treatment using a local anesthetic or no anesthetic at all (such as some eye cases or certain cases involving the removal of warts from feet) may be treated in the laser center. Patients whose surgery requires general anesthesia will receive laser treatment in an operating room.

Laser nurses may also be responsible for educating patients on the laser procedure—what to expect and how the healing process will go. They also assist surgeons during the laser part of an operation. They conduct workshops for nursing personnel, physicians, and biomedical technicians—a responsibility that may take up as much as 30 percent of their time. Approximately 20 percent more goes into public relations, such as speaking to various community groups, which leaves about half of the laser nurse's time for patient care (including surgery) and patient education.

A Typical Day

The day begins early. The laser nurse coordinator (LNC) arrives at work at 6:30 A.M. The first task is to check the surgical schedule to see what types of operations are going to be performed.

Robert described a day on which he found there were six laser operations scheduled in this way: "The first one was hemorrhoid surgery, with the CO_2 laser. Then there were two eye cases back-to-back. One was eye surgery to correct a condition that occasionally occurs after cataract surgery. We planned to use the Nd:YAG laser. The second was a panretinal photocoagulation to get rid of abnormal blood vessels that grow in the retina as a complication of diabetes—a procedure in which we would use the argon laser. Finally, there were three cases in a row in which we were destroying bladder tumors with a high-powered Nd:YAG laser."

For safety and security, and because some of the laser equipment costs more than $150,000, the treatment rooms containing them are kept locked. Robert, who described himself as "the keeper of the keys," unlocked the rooms to prepare them for the surgeries. Additionally, each laser is locked with a separate key, which the laser nurse carries.

Robert wheeled the laser into position, prepared the operating table by draping it, and opened up the instrument trays. He plugged the laser into its special electrical circuit, since it takes an immense amount of power. He wheeled in the smoke evacuator and set it up, to keep the air clear of vapor caused by the impact of the laser beam on tissue.

Robert made sure the medical records for each patient were laid out on the work table, ready for the doctor. Careful, detailed records are kept by the hospital's medical records department and are used for analysis and reference.

For each procedure, the physician records the power settings, the type of laser used, the amount of time the patient received laser treatment, how the laser beam was delivered to the tissue, the safety precautions taken to protect the patient, the verification of the patient's consent to operate, the type of operation performed, and the diagnosis of the patient's condition. The laser nurse coordinator checks and keeps a copy of all this information, and the records will be analyzed later.

The laser nurse coordinator is present at laser surgeries both in treatment rooms and in the hospital's operating room (OR). In the OR the laser nurse is scrubbed, gowned, masked, and gloved. After the patient has been put under general anesthesia, the LNC prepares the laser for use in a sterile field and places sterile drapes (or cloths) over the arm of the laser. The smoke evacuator is also draped to keep it sterile.

The physician tells the LNC what power setting will be used for the treatment and where he or she wants the laser beam delivered. Robert adjusts the laser accordingly, making sure it is set properly and functioning correctly.

As laser safety officer, the LNC also has the responsibility of checking that safety procedures are being followed during the surgery. Everyone, including the patient, must wear proper eye protection at all times. The patient's operative site will be covered with wet towels to protect the surrounding skin that isn't being treated. The LNC will make sure the doors to the operating room are shut, that warning signs are posted showing that laser surgery is going on, and that no one comes in or goes out. The LNC also makes sure there is always water available, if a fire should occur, and is prepared for other kinds of emergencies, such as power failure.

If anything in the room, or in procedures during the laser surgery, does not meet the LNC's safety standards or satisfaction, he or she has the authority to stop the treatment and immediately turn off the laser.

Hours, Salary, and Preparation

Hours for LNCs can be long. Even though normal working hours are usually from 6:30 A.M. to 3:00 P.M. Monday through Friday, with weekends off, they are on call for emergencies.

The salary for this position is approximately $45,000 to $50,000 a year. Assistants and technicians in laser centers receive somewhat less, usually earning from $32,000 to $43,000.

For a position as a nurse laser coordinator, a person must graduate and be licensed as a registered nurse. Certification as a laser coordinator can be earned in various ways through workshops and seminars as well as onsite classes. Continuing education hours will also be needed to meet individual standards of various hospitals.

Laser Coordinator in a Medical Center

A medical center laser coordinator's job is similar to an LNC's. Susan studied sociology at the University of South Dakota, from which she graduated with a bachelor's degree in 1976. She also earned an associate degree in nursing. For a time she worked as a registered nurse in South Dakota.

A move to a Denver, Colorado, hospital gave her nursing experience in liver transplants and intensive care. She did not enjoy rotating between day and night shifts, however, and, looking for stable hours, she moved to a nearby medical center. After three years of working in the recovery room, she helped set up the center's first outpatient surgical area.

"The center bought its first laser in 1983," Susan remembered. "Since I was the most interested, I volunteered to take courses and learn more about it. I wanted to get credentialed in laser safety and help train other nurses."

Susan's position as laser coordinator combined the administrative responsibilities of a laser safety officer with those of a clinical coordinator. She helped educate nurses on laser procedures. In addition, she was at the center for every laser surgery, making sure equipment was properly set up and all safety features were in place.

The medical center acquired a number of medical lasers, including a YAG laser and an argon laser for ophthalmology procedures, an argon laser for gynecological and dermatology surgery, two CO_2 lasers for general surgery, and a YAG laser with fiber-optic capabilities to be used for pulmonary, gynecological, and gastroenterological treatment.

When she prepares the operating rooms for surgery and checks the laser safety features, much of Susan's work is similar to that of a laser nurse coordinator in a hospital. She is also involved in a task force that is investigating how to start new laser programs for other procedures. "I spend a lot of time with vendors," she says, "because as soon as anyone hears you have a laser program, they want to sell you something. I spend much of my time doing physician marketing, explaining the lasers and helping the physicians arrange a trial run, setting up a practice session for them with the equipment. I troubleshoot when there are laser problems or problems with related equipment, working closely with our biomedical technician. The laser is a temperamental machine, and it's good to have a backup person."

It's a long day for Susan. She comes to work at 7:30 A.M. and often doesn't leave until 6:30 or 7:00 P.M. The medical center has just hired an assistant for her, which will ease the pressure.

Being relieved of some of the responsibility will free Susan to complete other projects, such as eye testing for staff personnel. Certain wavelengths, like that of the argon laser, can penetrate through the eye to the retina and damage patients' or staff members' eyes if a stray beam escapes or reflects. Susan makes sure all staff members who work with the lasers have received eye tests. Results are recorded in their personnel files. If they leave the center, their eyes will be tested again and records compared, to be sure they have not sustained any eye damage.

"Every day, I'm still finding out what my job is," Susan said. "It's a lot of hard work, but it's really rewarding."

Laser Educators

Many hospitals and medical centers offer laser courses to their own staff members, and others bring in outside consultants to perform that function. Educational services corporations put on such courses for national and international clients. These courses can range from a three-page self-learning booklet on a technique, product, or procedure to a one-day workshop, to a textbook or training manual, or a full five-day convention.

Some of these service companies specialize in particular areas. For instance, they may deal specifically with lasers in health care and operating room management. "We help hospitals look at their program," says one laser educator and the president of a Wisconsin-based company. "We make recommendations for what type of program they should be formulating. Then we give them a program description; write policies, procedures, and job descriptions; and help them implement the program."

The company presents hands-on, two-day workshops that help nursing staff members understand laser technology. In addition, the company acts as an all-round resource for clients on an ongoing basis, keeping them aware of changes in technology.

Hospitals are eager to hire trained employees. Because the technology changes rapidly, continuing education is important. Hospitals, community and four-year colleges, professional associations, manufacturers and distributors of equipment, and accrediting agencies offer a variety of courses for students online, in the classroom, and on the job.

Keeping up with new developments is a requirement of keeping certifications current.

Professional Certification and Organizations

The American Medical Technologists (AMT), certified by the National Commission of Certifying Agencies, is a national agency that certifies health practitioners as:

- Certified laboratory consultant (CLC)
- Certified medical administrative specialist (CMAS)
- Certified office laboratory technician (COLT)

- Medical laboratory technician (MLT)
- Medical technologist (MT)
- Registered dental assistant (RDA)
- Registered medical assistant (RMA)
- Registered phlebotomy technician (RPT)

Each one of these specialized medical areas requires familiarity and skill with one or more lasers of different kinds. The AMT provides complete information about certification and certification examinations in each of these career specialties, including schools, scholarships, legislative news, and continuing education. AMT state and student organizations and the national annual meeting provide opportunities for networking and keeping up to date as a professional in the field. Additional benefits of membership and a feature called "Career Connections" are presented on the agency's website.

For more information, contact:

American Medical Technologists
710 Higgins Road
Park Ridge, Ilinois 60068
www.amt1.com

Is a health care career working with lasers for you? Yes, say many current practitioners, if you like the medical environment, are willing to work hard, and are interested in keeping up with technological developments. Medical research is moving so quickly that continuing your education is a must in this demanding profession.

Both of the major umbrella associations in medical and dental care can also supply additional information about requirements in their fields.

American Medical Association (AMA)
515 North State Street
Chicago, Ilinois 60611
www.ama.org

American Dental Association (ADA)
211 East Chicago Avenue
Chicago, Ilinois 60611
www.ada.org

4

Lasers in Manufacturing

From the CDs and DVDs, computer laser mouses, and bar code scanners that we encounter each day, to the laser beams used by NASA to measure distance in space, lasers are being applied to hundreds of uses. Not only do lasers operate within these countless gadgets and high-tech miracles, they are often used to actually build the products themselves.

The uses of lasers in manufacturing have certain advantages over traditional manufacturing processes. The special properties of laser light (monochromaticity, coherence, divergence, and brightness) make lasers particularly useful for many industrial practices, such as the following.

- Cladding
- Cutting
- Drilling

- Heat treating
- Marking
- Welding

Cladding is a technique used to melt alloys and selectively deposit them onto the surfaces of parts. You are probably already familiar with the basics of the other functions listed. Lasers also are used to strip wires, drill tiny holes for watch jewels, and even cut cloth for the mass production of clothing.

When people imagine having careers with lasers in manufacturing, they often picture themselves standing at a table, aiming a laser beam at the items they want to cut or weld. In today's factories, however, the laser is rarely a stand-alone machine. It is usually part of an automated process, one that frequently involves computers and a number of highly coordinated and automatic steps, perhaps even involving robots.

A laser manufacturing system needs a way of delivering the part to the workstation for the laser operation and of taking the part away to the next stop after the laser process has been completed.

The process also calls for a laser system capable of generating sufficient energy to perform the desired task and a way of focusing the laser beam to deliver the energy to the right spot on the part (a task often handled by automated vision systems).

Since only part of the electrical energy can be used as optical output (the laser beam), a laser manufacturing system needs a cooling system to get rid of the rest of the energy and resulting heat. If the laser process involves removing or vaporizing material (such as in drilling or cutting operations), an exhaust system is needed to remove smoke, gas, and particles of material from the workstation.

The manufacturing system involving lasers will also usually have a controller to make sure everything is happening for the required length of time and in the required sequence. An off-line programming system is often used so that changes in the computer program governing the operation can take place without having to shut down the assembly process.

Although industrial lasers have been in use for several decades, their popularity in the last fifteen or twenty years has surged, as more and more factories turn to high-tech processes. Initially, laser equipment vendors supplied turnkey systems. Even today, the capital investment required for installing a large, powerful laser system is significant—often more than $750,000. However, the continually improving technology has dropped the cost for certain kinds of lasers. Consequently, smaller factories are finding lasers affordable and are beginning to install one or more for "job shop" or custom work.

Advantages of Lasers

Although the initial cost may be high, and time must be dedicated to training workers to use lasers safely and properly, lasers are still very economical. They have several advantages over other manufacturing techniques.

In traditional manufacturing processes such as welding, cutting, and drilling, tools come in contact with the parts being worked on. Friction and the abrasive contact between tool and part wear out machine tools, so they must be replaced often. Tool replacement is much less frequent with lasers, because the beam is performing machining operations without direct contact.

Because the laser beam can be precisely focused, the energy needed to accomplish the work can be placed very accurately. In addition, very little of the material surrounding the site of the laser weld or laser cut is affected by the heat resulting from the energy that's delivered. Consequently, the material being worked on has less damage and waste. In traditional machining, sometimes as much as 90 percent of the original piece of metal is whittled away. Not so with lasers. Parts are less deformed. That's an important advantage when work is being performed on parts for an aircraft engine or when lasers are being used in small welded assembly jobs.

Flexibility is another advantage of laser processing. By changing its settings, it is possible to control the heat and energy of the laser to give the beam more or less power, as desired.

Engineers can quickly design specifications on their computers and transmit the instructions to the laser. This is far more efficient than waiting for the assembly line to be retooled. Now companies can alter the design of a product, make upgrades, and respond to changes in market demand quickly and affordably.

Speed is another important advantage of using lasers. In many cases lasers can process materials at a substantially faster rate than more traditional methods. The line moves faster, thus saving money.

Laser tooling often also has the advantage of simplifying a job. Most lasers have multi-axis capability—that is, they can be positioned to work in different directions. If a part is round, or if laser work (such as a weld) must be done at a difficult angle, the laser tool can usually handle the job. Because the laser beam can be focused to a very small diameter, lasers can work on areas of parts that otherwise would be harder to reach. One company uses lasers to manufacture golf tees, perfectly turning out the tiny rounded contours in a fraction of the time it would take using traditional methods.

Types of Lasers

Many different kinds of lasers are used, in a great variety of applications. Some of the many kinds of lasers in use today are:

- Carbon dioxide
- Copper vapor
- Dye
- Excimer
- Fiber
- HeNe
- Ion
- Nd: YAG
- Nitrogen
- OPOs
- Quantum cascade
- Ruby
- Semiconductor
- Terahertz sources
- Ti:Sa
- Ultra-short pulses

A solid-state laser uses a crystal for the lasing medium. A gas laser, such as a carbon dioxide laser (CO_2 laser) uses the gas as the lasing medium.

Some lasers, such as the neodymium-doped yttrium aluminum garnet laser (Nd:YAG) and the CO_2 laser, can be operated to produce a continuous wave. Others, such as the ruby laser and neodymium-doped-glass laser (Nd:glass laser) are set up to provide short pulses of laser light. The Nd:YAG and CO_2 lasers also can be operated as pulsed lasers, if that mode is appropriate for the material-handling process. The solid-state alexandrite laser is another such laser that can operate either in a pulsed mode or as a continuous wave.

The choice of the particular type of laser to use depends on a number of factors, including the power range needed to perform the desired task. For example, YAG lasers are well suited for precision drilling and cutting operations on a wide variety of inorganic materials where power ranges of 0.5 kilowatts or less are required. YAG lasers have two important advantages over conventional tools in these applications. The laser beam does not get dull or change its size or shape as a result of wear. In addition, the way the laser beam performs is not substantially affected by degree of hardness or machinability of the piece the laser is working on.

Different lasers provide different advantages in manufacturing. CO_2 lasers provide a powerhouse for industry. They're able to operate at high power levels, often making them the technology of choice for heavy-duty industrial applications like cutting, welding, and heat treating. The CO_2 laser is also well suited for processing many organic materials.

Just as CO_2 lasers supply high power, YAG lasers are often chosen for applications needing lower power. YAG laser systems have successfully drilled a wide variety of high-temperature alloy aircraft turbine components, automotive gear, bearing materials, and other precision parts. They are also used for cutting complex shapes in products ranging from steel automobile doors to titanium aircraft components and for welding a variety of industrial products.

Carbon dioxide laser applications include cutting and welding a variety of metals of different thicknesses; cutting, drilling, and welding plastics and such other organic materials as leather, wood, and paper; cutting and drilling glass, quartz, ceramics, and similar materials; and heat treating and surface treating a variety of metals. If desired, a CO_2 laser can be attached to a robot manipulator and used for production welding, cutting, heat treating, and similar applications.

A YAG laser and CO_2 laser can be combined on the same laser processing system for additional flexibility. Both the YAG laser and the CO_2 units can be permanently attached and can share the same delivery system for the laser beam. Or both laser units can be configured and installed as stand-alone units, so that the YAG laser and CO_2 laser have individual delivery systems.

Vendors work closely with factory engineers and process planners to match laser characteristics to application requirements in order to achieve maximum efficiency in a highly cost-effective installation.

Raycon Corporation, which is a world leader in the manufacture of custom laser processing systems, is especially involved in auto manufacturing and the aerospace industry. In one instance, a manufacturer of jet engines needed a laser machine tool that would work well with different aerospace metals, different-shaped parts that were being processed, parts that varied in size, and different processing applications. There was no room for error in finished parts; the machining tolerances were exacting, and the parts in work had to be held completely secure in position so the laser beam could be focused precisely on the required point.

Raycon worked to develop a laser processing system that was both versatile and precise, while meeting the particular application requirements. Similar systems are designed and installed for other manufacturers, and they too are built with flexibility so they can be modified, either with commercially available equipment or with custom-made hardware and software.

Resources for Learning More About Industrial Lasers

Many different kinds of resources are available for finding more information about the work environments in the laser industry. The websites of hundreds of corporations on the Internet, professional organizations and associations, trade shows and conventions, and books and periodicals all provide a wealth of information. Many of the books listed in the Further Reading section at the end of this book have information on various laser applications.

Technical Articles

Current technical articles about "Lasers in Manufacturing" are listed in the *Applied Science and Technology Index*, which can be found on the Internet and on reference shelves in almost every public library.

Professional Papers

An excellent source for papers on lasers in manufacturing is the Society of Manufacturing Engineers, One SME Drive, P.O. Box 930, Dearborn, Michigan 48121, or at www.sme.org on the Internet. You can e-mail or write the publications department for the current catalog, which lists books, videos, CD-ROMs and DVDs, training programs, and technical journals published by SME.

By searching the publications list, you will find hundreds of publications that contain information on lasers. Such papers as "Laser Selection for Drilling" and "Laser Selection for Cutting" give specific information about particular laser applications. Reading papers like these will help you learn more about lasers in manufacturing and will give you a chance to see if a career in that field appeals to you.

Meetings and Conferences

One way to learn more about lasers in manufacturing is to attend the conferences and meetings of the major professional societies and associations. On the local level, both student and professional chapters of SME hold meetings at which speakers present topics.

Major trade shows, conventions, and expositions, where you will see hundreds of people, visit information booths of organizations, listen to featured speakers, and gather a great deal of knowledge in a short time, are one of the most exciting ways to gain an overview of a field.

SME and SPIE—the International Society for Optical Engineering—and others sponsor large trade shows several times a year. Examples are FABTECH International & AWS Welding, held at the McCormick Place Exposition Center in Chicago in 2007, and the Advanced Manufacturing Expo in Canada in 2008.

Major conventions like these can expect to draw many thousands of professionals and students and will last for several days. They provide workshops and seminars, as well as less formal opportunities for learning abut the field. Additional associations and societies, important schools, and research institutes will be represented by booths and/or speakers. Often, a career center or an actual in-show job fair will be arranged to allow people to network and meet potential employees and employers.

Smaller meetings in local or regional areas often provide good speakers and clinics and discussion of key topics. Papers presented at these clinics may provide case studies of laser systems at individual firms ("Microelectronic Laser Welding: Proven on the Production Floor") or offer discussions of technical and economic aspects of laser work ("Process in Laser Marking and Engraving").

Multimedia Resources

DVDs, CDs, films, slide presentations, and videos are available to show you various laser manufacturing processes in action. SME and SPIE both have extensive libraries of materials for individual viewing. Case studies demonstrate how using lasers can improve manufacturing productivity and profitability, and self-paced interactive courses are available for individual research and, in some cases, for continuing education credits.

SME also has multimedia materials that are available for schools, career counselors, and libraries. For more information contact the SME education department.

Kinds of Jobs and Income Levels

Several levels of jobs are available for people who want to work with lasers in manufacturing. The specific job titles may vary from company to company, and duties may sometimes overlap or vary slightly. Nevertheless, the basic job names and categories that follow are recognizable across the industry in the United States and Canada and most other countries.

Operators

In many laser manufacturing centers, there is a substantial need for people who are "doers" and whose knowledge of lasers is focused upon a very specific function. Often men and women who physically operate lasers in manufacturing have come from other manufacturing backgrounds. Perhaps they have been numerical control operators with previous experience in running controllers that oversee automated operations. With previous training and experience in machining or in tool and die work, these specialists can begin to operate lasers after relatively minimal additional training.

This training can often be carried out by detailed interactive graphics and often on-site at the factory location. Ford Motor Company has used such training, and the operator watches a computer screen on which questions appear. If the worker gives the correct answer, he or she continues to the next question; if not, the screen displays an animated character who indicates the mistake and provides additional learning material.

As of 2004, the latest year for which Department of Labor statistics were available for this area at publication time for this book, median salaries at this level were $14.70 per hour, $11.00 or $12.00 per hour in a small job shop, and up to $15.43 an hour or higher in the automotive and aerospace industries.

Laser Equipment Maintenance Workers

The next level up from operations is laser equipment maintenance. The worker will usually be required to have taken at least a two-year educational program about laser principles, applications, operations, and safety. The maintenance worker will clean portions of the laser system periodically and replace worn parts. Usually the duties are limited to following a checklist, doing the items as predetermined. For example, one task might be to "take out the lens and clean it." Another might be "check filter."

After the maintenance worker removes and replaces a lens, he or she has to test the machine to see if it was replaced correctly. Maintenance also includes the cooling systems, and the worker must be trained in maintaining certain types of refrigeration. Most of the knowledge and skills needed are taught at the two-year college level in technician and technology programs.

The salary level in 2004 was from approximately $9.21 up to $21.90 an hour for maintenance people, and many higher paid workers were likely to belong to a union.

Service Specialists

Service personnel—at another level higher than maintenance people—are usually employed by equipment or service vendors and visit customer sites to fix problems or troubleshoot the laser system. They are also called *service representatives*, or *service reps*.

These specialists are detectives. Although they listen to what operators and maintenance people tell them about why the laser doesn't seem to work properly, a service representative has to decide whether those people are really good observers or are merely passing on preconceived ideas. Service personnel need to work well under pressure and time deadlines—often from both their own employers and from plant management. Very often they will have to stand before a meeting of the company's managers or even the board of directors to explain just why the expensive laser system isn't working.

Service reps need real ability to solve problems. They must make their own independent observations of manufacturing processes, see what problems are happening, and try to clear them up quickly and economically. To identify problems, causes, and remedies, service reps must know how to use typical electronic diagnostic tools, such as meters and scopes and analytical optical equipment.

Salaries for service reps run from approximately $23,000 to $52,000 per year. Extensive travel may be involved, because service is performed at the clients' plants, wherever they are located. Some travel may be outside the United States.

Applications Engineers

Above service personnel in this informal hierarchy are applications engineers. Often these are service personnel who have earned engineering degrees and have been promoted to these positions. They are usually employed by the laser manufacturer (the vendor of laser equipment) to work with potential clients before the sale is made—defining the client's needs and working out a good fit with the manufacturer's products.

Applications engineers need a combination of technical knowledge and sales orientation, along with good listening skills and the ability to make good presentations.

These people usually are required to have earned a four-year degree, possibly from a technical college, in engineering, physics, electronics, mechanical design, or a related discipline. Speaking and writing abilities are vital, because the applications engineer must be able to hold his or her own in management arguments and must, in fact, help to convince the client company that the vendor's product is the right one to buy. Even though the applications engineer is not always officially part of the vendor's sales team, he or she plays an important role in making the sale. Applications engineers must be able to identify the customer's problems and needs and come up with workable solutions utilizing the vendor's products to make them feasible.

Salaries for applications engineers are in the $30,000 range for those just beginning their careers at this level. Experienced applications engineers may receive between $49,000 and $85,000, with an average being about $67,000 per year. In most cases, they work as salaried employees and not on commission.

Laser Scientists

Slightly higher than the salary level of an applications engineer, but probably working in a corporate research laboratory rather than for a vendor of laser equipment, is a laser scientist. Laser scientists have a laser science background. A typical task in this job might involve matching a laser to a robot. The laser scientist will work out the plan for the project and may supervise a team in developing a model. Responsibilities may include planning, research, plan modification at various stages, drawing up a proposal, budgeting, meeting deadlines, making presentations to management and manufacturing staff, as well as sales and service representatives when the product is ready for presentation to the market.

Earnings for laser scientists have a broad range but, in general, the median wage can be expected to be about $72,000, with the lowest being about $40,000 and the highest being as much as $113,000 per year.

A few laser scientists are employed by companies that evaluate acquisitions—they provide the service of evaluations for other people who are in the business of buying and selling laser companies.

Sales Representatives

The salesperson, also known as the *field representative* or *field engineer*, is often a design engineer in terms of educational background. Employed by the laser equipment vendor, this person must almost always have an engineering degree from a four-year school. Added to that is a strong business orientation, including knowledge of business law, marketing techniques, and business administration. Although the salesperson does not necessarily have to come up the ladder of experience as a service person and applications engineer, many of them have. Such a person has picked up business law and marketing expertise—perhaps in night school courses—after acquiring the technical education and experience.

The median salary for a field representative or sales engineer was $70,620 in 2004, according to Department of Labor statistics. The range was from $41,430 at the low end to $117,260 at the high end. Sales engineers often receive the use of company cars, expenses, and commissions on new sales. Substantial salary increases may also be earned with advancement to regional or district sales manager or beyond.

Laser/Electro-Optical Product Engineers

Under the supervision of the product manager–lasers, this person is responsible for the engineering concerned with the YAG and CO_2 lasers and associated laser equipment that is incorporated in the company's machine tool product lines. This means involvement in the quotation stage to recommend a laser product that would satisfy the customer's needs, as well as recommending and overseeing mechanical and electrical design details that are associated with the incorporation of the laser into the machine tool product.

Additional associated duties include documentation of design efforts. The person holding this position must generate design specifications, test specifications, and test reports. In addition, the laser/electro-optical product engineer must generate quality control procedures, safety procedures, and service procedures.

Other duties in this position include assembling and generating mechanical and electrical drawings, a parts list, and user and maintenance manuals for the laser and associated laser equipment. Other people may help with the drawings and manuals if the machine tool's operation overlaps that of the laser.

To qualify as a laser/electro-optical product engineer, the person holding the job should have a bachelor of science degree in electrical engineering with an emphasis on electro-optics. In addition, four years of experience with laser equipment is required. One year's experience should be with the integration of lasers and machine tools. This product engineer will have had laser training at various manufacturers' locations and, preferably, schooling in computer numerical control.

Product Design Engineers

Holding a position comparable to that of the district sales manager (and earning approximately the same compensation) is a product design engineer, sometimes called an *advance design engineer*. Such a person has a university degree and may also have completed graduate work in engineering. He or she may work for a vendor or may be a scientist/entrepreneur who owns a small laser company. Salary levels for this position can range from $50,000 to well over $100,000 per year.

Job Qualifications

Although these jobs and their levels of involvement may have slightly different names in different companies, you can be sure that each company has a job description that describes these basic desired qualifications.

For the purposes of this book, one corporate sales director has provided three examples of qualifications used by his company. By reading them, you'll have an idea of the knowledge and skills that the persons holding those jobs are actually required to have.

1. **Laser product technician.** A person who could satisfy the required qualifications for this position would:

   - Be able to read circuit diagrams and blueprints
   - Have a general mechanical/electrical aptitude
   - Have or be able to develop a knowledge of the primary process for which the machine was developed and be able to optimize that process
   - Work in the assembly area, preparing the machine for delivery and run-off

2. **Laser applications technician.** A person who could satisfy the required qualifications for this position would:

   - Become very familiar with a machine's capabilities and be able to use those capabilities in a variety of applications
   - Have a working knowledge of computer numerically controlled (CNC) equipment and machine tools

- Have a complete knowledge of CNC programming and be able to exercise the machine to its full capability
- Have metrological and metalography knowledge for determination of laser sample dimensional and process quality
- Have excellent computer knowledge for organizing data and posting results
- Be working in the applications lab

3. **Laser field technician/engineer.** A person who could satisfy the requirements for this position would:

- Read circuit diagrams and blueprints
- Be able to troubleshoot industrial electrical and electronic equipment on a module/board level
- Have good general mechanical/electrical aptitude
- Have a working knowledge of and be able to perform basic troubleshooting on a variety of machine CNCs
- Have good computer working knowledge for posting such items as repair requirements, hours, and parts replaced
- Be working in the field at the customer's site

Each of the jobs described above also requires a comprehensive knowledge of laser safety. Persons holding these jobs must have a working knowledge of industrial lasers and be able to remove and clean optical components, align the laser optical resonator for peak output, adjust focusing optics, operate the laser controller, and change flashlamps or discharge tubes for both solid-state and gas lasers.

Laser Machinist

In Arizona, thirty-six-year-old Rick had more than nine years of experience working at an aerospace corporation. The story of how he was chosen for his position in the company's development department illustrates one example of working your way up to running a laser.

As a teenager, Rick spent his last two high school years at a technical school. After graduation, the school helped him get a job at a factory in a nearby city.

The options of three training programs were offered. Gear grinding and boring mills paid the best, but he was looking for the technology of the future. Numerical control (NC) machines were just starting up, and he thought he could get in on the ground floor. Rick trained on NC drilling and boring machines, and he got a good background.

Because he was young and not ready to settle down, he left the factory and spent several years working his way around the country, taking whatever jobs he could find. By the time he was married and expecting his first child, he had settled in Phoenix, hiring on at what was then called Garrett Engine Turbines.

After a year, he had worked his way up from manual drills to NC machines. His technical school background and previous work experience helped him get the promotion.

Three years later, the company planned to put in a laser machining center. The idea of learning new technology had always been challenging and had served Rick well. Long before the laser actually arrived, he asked to be assigned to it. When it came in, he was given the chance to work with it.

Eventually, Rick was assigned to work with an Nd:YAG pulsed laser used for cutting applications. In the company's research department, workers were also testing a high-powered CO_2 laser for heat-related processing.

In his job, Rick generally worked six days a week, from 7:00 A.M. to 3:00 or 3:30 P.M. When he arrived, he would start up the console; loading up the software sometimes took long enough for Rick to get a cup of coffee. By the time he returned, the machine's power supply had turned itself on and was warming up the circuits.

Next Rick would reference the laser. He needed to align the laser beam at the exact reference spot from which all cutting dimensions were determined. A nozzle assembly on the machine held the focusing optics that controlled the laser beam. That assembly would ride up and down on a worm screw. The laser nozzle itself had no rotating parts.

To help position the machine, Rick hooked up a TV camera to run along the same path as the laser beam when it was machining. The TV screen was mounted right on the same assembly as the console. On the screen, Rick could see electronic crosshairs that helped him place the beam in just the right spot.

To reference the machine, Rick positioned it over a piece of scrap metal. He could place the machine precisely—within about one ten-thousandth of an inch of where he wanted it to be. Then he fired a single shot (or pulse of energy) with the laser to mark the metal part. The TV screen showed where the laser beam hit. Rick needed to align the site hole to the electronic crosshairs on the TV screen. Once he had matched them exactly, he had a reference point.

The instructions for the machine, regarding exactly where the laser beam would cut, were based on the distances from that reference point. Those instructions had been worked out beforehand and programmed into NC tape. The tape went through a tape reader, and the instructions were stored in the CNC microprocessor that ran the laser. Because the instructions could be retrieved and loaded into the computer's memory, Rick could modify the program if necessary, just as a secretary might edit a letter whose text had been stored in a word-processing program.

The company's programming department usually wrote the software programs that informed Rick's laser exactly where and how to cut the metal engine parts. That was because his machine used two and three axes simultaneously, as it made the cuts in the metal engine parts. Rick, however, had enough computer knowledge to modify the program or to write one himself if the programming department was backed up.

Although much of Rick's computer programming knowledge was picked up on the job, he learned a lot from a CNC programming course that was run by Arizona State University and taught to company machinists at their request. His company was very education oriented. He was also taking additional college courses to become more familiar with specialized materials and processing techniques.

Because Rick worked in the company's development department, he handled a number of innovative designs from different divisions. His group received parts not only from one department but from all over the plant. Since the company made engine parts for airplanes such as Lear jets, Rick sometimes tested the practicality of laser cutting on everything from research combustors with thousands of holes to sheet-metal casings for the engine with perhaps thirty holes to gears that needed clearance holes drilled into them.

Rick's supervisor assigned priorities and planned Rick's approximate schedule, but no two days were ever the same. Sometimes he spent 90 percent of his time running the laser, making the cuts as desired. Other days he encountered problems and had to take time to solve them, which slowed down his output.

Each metal that Rick worked with, from titanium to the exotic alloys used in aerospace manufacturing, had its own characteristics, which could vary according to the grade of metal or alloy used. Rick adjusted the laser to achieve optimum cutting performance for each of them.

Rick observed safety precautions, including shielding for the engine parts, since molten material is ejected from the laser cut. Rick would wear laser safety glasses for the specific wavelength of his Nd:YAG pulsed laser. They had been ground to his prescription, so he did not have to wear laser safety goggles over his prescription lenses. The special glasses protected his eyes from stray laser light and reflection. Like all company workers, he also wore safety shoes, a standard requirement in manufacturing.

The salary or wages for a job like Rick's, combining elements of operation, maintenance, service, and some occasional programming and modifications, would likely bring a salary of $26,000 to $45,000 a year, based on the length of service and the person's qualifications. With additional training and continuing education, the salary level would be likely to increase.

In some places this job would be a union job, and, in that case, union wages, benefits, and rules would apply. The machinists' union is the International Association of Machinists and Aerospace Workers (IAMAW). For more information about the union, go to www.goiam.org.

Research Engineer

Patrick, a senior manufacturing research engineer, worked at a corporate research and engineering center in Michigan in advanced manufacturing engineering and advanced product development and research. He spent approximately a fourth of his time working on lasers.

A former faculty instructor in welding at the University of Wisconsin–Madison, Patrick was familiar with the ruby laser in the university's mechanical engineering department and suggested to the corporate research center that it could be used in process development work.

At the research and development facility, the Nd:YAG solid-state and CO_2 gas lasers were both used. At the plants, low-powered helium-neon (HeNe) lasers read bar codes and were part of scanning systems used to check the quality of prepainted steel. The company used two CO_2 lasers at different plant locations for welding parts for making automatic washing machines. One laser welded a gear assembly. The other welded a stamped bracket to the tube that spun the washing machine's basket.

Patrick said that no one worked only with lasers as their job. Once a laser system was in place in a plant, the laser became a part of several people's responsibilities. In one location, a process or manufacturing engineer might have it, with a person under the engineer doing secondary machining operations. In another location, the welding engineer might take responsibility for a laser.

At the plant, the laser operator might check tools and specifically check parts, but the actual loading and unloading of parts to the laser workstation was automatic. The operator watched the overall machinery—one piece of which was the laser. Since the laser was simple to run, an operator could bring the system up quickly. Usually the laser required little attention. Periodic maintenance involved cleaning and replacing the optical components and, for the CO_2 laser, changing the bottles of gas.

The lasers represented a major capital investment for the manufacturer. Depending on the complexity of the equipment, the cost might go as high as a quarter of a million dollars or more.

When lasers are chosen for a particular manufacturing application, they're usually installed to solve a special problem. "Companies can't cost-effectively install a laser to replace a conventional operation that works well," Patrick noted, "but it might provide a savings on cost of material. For instance, one gear assembly replaced a part made on a screw machine from a solid bar. We chose the CO_2 laser because it was the only way to make that particular gear assembly in two pieces and then put it together. In the welding application, laser welding has a low heat input. Using the CO_2 laser eliminated distortion and gave the manufacturer quality improvement."

Researching Laser Jobs in Manufacturing

Because manufacturing applications of lasers are constantly progressing to new and better technology, it is a good idea to keep informed. Unions, professional associations, trade shows, meetings, workshops, and seminars are all useful for keeping up on developments. Corporate websites provide up-to-date information on companies' products, job openings, and publications.

A sample of corporations in the industry is provided here. Take a look at the variety of services and products that they provide, and you will note that some specialize in highly focused, customized applications, while others provide broad ranges of products and services. Obviously, this is only a small group, provided as a sample— you will want to research more extensively on your own to discover the many progressive companies with state-of-the-art applications and opportunities.

- **Alabama Laser, Munford, Alabama.** Custom industrial lasers: marking systems, including CO_2 and Nd:YAG lasers; fiber-delivered, direct diode lasers; fiber and green lasers
- **Automated Laser Corporation, Fort Wayne, Indiana.** CO_2 lasers for marking systems; complete and production-ready products; highest durability
- **Clark-MXR Inc., Dexter, Michigan.** Cutting-edge, ultrafast industrial lasers, systems, and welding; provides micromachines and diode lasers with ultrafast technology capabilities
- **Continuum, Santa Clara, California.** Nd:YAG lasers, OPOs (optical parametric oscillators), dye and custom laser systems, pulsed solid-state lasers, novel YAG configurations, tunable laser systems
- **Corry Laser Technology Inc., Corry, Pennsylvania.** Specialty shop for laser machining; laser cutting, marking, welding, CO_2 lasers and laser drilling. Work with aerospace alloys, ceramics, and so forth
- **DD Wire Company Inc., Temple City, California.** Wide range of metal processing: heavy plate processing to fine detail laser cutting; work with metals and nonmetals for cutting, stamping, forming
- **EBTEC Corporation, Agawan, Massachusetts.** Precision laser cutting services; CNC laser cutting, welding, and drilling
- **Engraving Systems Integrators Inc., Cleveland, Ohio.** Industrial lasers: laser marking systems and cutting machines for engrav-

ing, cutting, marking; computerized laser engraving and cutting systems; and desktop laser engravers

- **Epilog Laser, Golden, Colorado.** Laser marking systems; CO_2 and diode lasers; laser cutting machines and systems for laser engraving, including tabletop, mid-sized, large-format engraving systems
- **LASAG Industrial Lasers USA, Buffalo Grove, Illinois.** Worldwide, Nd:YAG lasers for materials processing; marking and welding lasers; machines for cutting, drilling, and ablating
- **Laser Services Inc., Westford, Massachusetts.** High-quality laser machining and laser-cutting services
- **Laservall North America LLC, Pawtucket, Rhode Island.** Nd:YAG lasers, marking lasers, diode lasers, and laser technology; new addition to the Laservall SPA group
- **New Wave Research Inc., Fremont, California.** Small pulsed Nd:YAG lasers, diode lasers, and laser systems used in a variety of applications, including LED manufacturing and microelectronics
- **Raycon Corporation, Ann Arbor, Michigan.** Custom small-hole EDM and laser processing systems, turnkey operations built to customer requirements for automotive and aerospace industries
- **RMI Laser LLC, Lafayette, Colorado.** Industrial DPSS lasers and turnkey laser marking systems; YVO4 technology; RMI lasers for marking, logos; 2D/UID codes on composites, plastics, and metals
- **Schmidt Marking Systems, Niles, Illinois.** ISO 9001:2000 certified; 5w–120w laser marking systems with 2D data matrix, bar coding, vision system capabilities. Systems: Nd:YAG, CO_2, fiber lasers
- **Sierra Laser Center, Anaheim, California.** Precision laser cutting services, through materials from 1.00-inch to .001-inch thickness, plus shapes, angles, and tubes

- **Synrad Inc. Mukilteo, Washington.** Sealed CO_2 lasers; evolution lasers for welding thin film, perform kiss-cuts and semiconductor wafer processing; Firestar series 100- and 200-watt lasers
- **Tecnar Automation Ltée, St-Bruno, Quebec.** On-contact laser ultrasonics; inspection systems (LUS); detection units such as pulsed, TWM, and Fabry-Perot cavity (FPC)
- **Telesis Technologies Inc., Circleville, Ohio.** Custom engineered and standard marking systems; Nd:YAG, CO_2, fiber, and diode-pumped equipment for industrial, health and medical, and consumer product applications
- **Will-Mann Inc., Fullerton, California.** High-quality sheet metal laser cutting, marking, welding services; CNC laser service, shearing, and braking; precision cutting and marking

This small sample of employers in the laser manufacturing field represents locations in Alabama, California, Colorado, Illinois, Indiana, Massachusetts, Michigan, Ohio, Pennsylvania, Rhode Island, and Washington, as well as Canada. The industry is widespread, and its locations are to be found not only in North America but throughout the world.

5

LASERS IN MILITARY AND SPACE APPLICATIONS

IN THE WAR in Iraq, the United States and other forces have used laser technology primarily in surveillance and identification of targets and in aiming missiles and other small weapons and bombs. No sooner had laser technology been invented than military leaders envisioned some of the possibilities for military applications. As early as 1965, the United States Army was developing a laser range finder.

Because laser light can be used to measure distances extremely accurately, airplanes and tanks are often equipped with laser range finders. Often, the Nd:YAG laser is used, sending out pulses of light to the target. When these pulses, which are invisible to the human eye, hit the target, they are reflected back to the sender. A computer carried by the airplane or tank can measure the time it took the pulses of light to make the round-trip and can then calculate the distance to the target. Smaller range finders have been developed that can be carried by individual soldiers working as forward observers. Soldiers equipped with individual range finders can provide distance readings to long-range artillery gunners. In civilian life, state highway patrol and local police use similar range finders to accurately track and time speeding cars.

Strategic Defense Initiative

One of the more well-known instances of the military development of laser technology was for the Strategic Defense Initiative (SDI). SDI was a U.S. military research program for developing an antiballistic missile (ABM) defense system that was first announced by President Ronald Reagan in a speech in 1983. The concept of SDI was a radical break with the nuclear strategy that had governed U.S. military policy since the development of the arms race. The system that Reagan proposed would provide a layered defense of the United States using futuristic weapons, some of which were only in the earliest stages of development. The idea behind SDI was that the proposed weapons, which included space- and ground-based nuclear x-ray lasers, subatomic particle beams, and automated space vehicles, would intercept incoming missiles high above Earth. Supporting the weapons would have been a network of space-based sensors and specialized mirrors for directing the laser beams toward targets, and the entire operation was to be controlled by a supercomputer.

The plan also called for space-contained laser battle stations. Each battle station would consist of an assembly of laser devices put together in modules. Once these stations were placed in orbit, they could engage ballistic missiles launched from anywhere on Earth, including those launched from submarines and intermediate-range ballistic missiles.

The direct energy weapons technology for SDI called for the space-based lasers to identify or destroy decoys while they were still in mid-flight and to defend U.S. satellites. Since the beam of some types of space-based lasers could penetrate the atmosphere down to the tops of clouds, it was hoped that the space-based lasers would help defend the United States against missiles sent from aircraft and from tactical ballistic missiles.

Since 1970, Department of Defense researchers had been working on chemical lasers fueled with hydrogen fluoride for possible use as space-based lasers. Such lasers operate in the infrared section of the electromagnetic spectrum at wavelengths of 2.7 micrometers.

Other possibilities for space-based lasers were devices that generate beams at short wavelengths of about a micrometer or less. Because brightness increases in a ratio of 1/wavelength square, being able to use shorter wavelengths can make the laser light much brighter, if the quality of the optics and the accuracy in aiming the laser are also increased proportionally. Two of these lasers with shorter wavelengths are the radio-frequency-linear accelerator free electron laser and the short-wavelength chemical laser. In another approach, researchers have worked with nuclear reactors to pump (or increase the strength of) a short-wavelength laser.

The Strategic Defense Initiative was nicknamed "Star Wars" after the popular 1977 science-fiction film. It was seen by its critics as unrealistic and even dangerous. In an April 1987 debate between General James Abrahamson, director of the Strategic Defense Initiative Organization, and noted astronomer Dr. Carl Sagan, director of the Laboratory for Planetary Studies at Cornell University,

Sagan called SDI "an immensely dangerous and foolish scheme." According to Sagan, 70 to 90 percent of the members of the National Academy of Sciences in the relevant disciplines of mathematics, physics, and engineering said that SDI would not work. SDI was also extremely expensive. The original projections ranged from $100 billion to $1 trillion.

One of the rationales behind SDI, besides its protective function, was that scientists in the Soviet Union were working on lasers powerful enough to destroy low-orbiting American satellites and damage those farther away. There was also concern that once SDI began to be implemented, the Soviet Union would develop its own lasers to threaten the U.S. satellites in the program.

A report in 1985 by the U.S. Department of Defense and the Department of State said that the Soviet Union's laser program already employed more than ten thousand scientists and engineers conducting research in the three types of gas laser considered most promising for weapons applications:

1. Gas-dynamic laser
2. Electric discharge laser
3. Chemical laser

The Soviets also were said to be working on short wavelength, excimer, free-electron, argon-ion, and x-ray lasers.

Ballistic Missile Defense Organization

With the dissolution of the Soviet Union in the early 1990s, however, the signing of a series of arms control treaties, and the election of Bill Clinton as president in 1992, the budget for the Strategic Defense Initiative was cut back. In 1993, under the direction of Defense Secretary Les Aspin, the Ballistic Missile Defense Organization (BMDO) was established in place of the SDI. Instead of using costly space-based defense weapons, BMDO relied on ground-based antimissile systems. Following the curtailing of SDI, more emphasis was placed on the concept of ground-based lasers to track and hit missiles. While the budget for SDI had been literally astronomical, actual expenditures amounted to about $30 billion. In contrast, the initial annual budget for BMDO was $3.8 billion.

The Ballistic Missile Defense Organization is central to the effort to uncover the military potential of lasers, and work on lasers also is being conducted by other branches of the armed forces. By the late 1990s, the BMDO program had created most of the key elements necessary for deploying a space-based laser, or SBL, which would be one of the most advanced defense weapons ever designed. It includes a high-energy beam generator named Alpha. Since 1991, Alpha has performed megawatt-class lasing in numerous tests, and by 1999 it was performing at near-weapons-class efficiency.

Another laser-related initiative was the Large Optics Demonstration Experiment initiated in 1987, and the four-meter-diameter Large Advanced Mirror Program (LAMP) in 1989. Since then, tests have been ongoing on improved mirrors and optics. The high-energy beam LAMP mirror is the largest mirror ever constructed for space use (the Hubble mirror measured 2.4 meters). The goal of the BMDO is to integrate the high-power chemical laser components with other technologies being deployed in space. Thus, one experiment entitled the Alpha Lamp Integration experiment involved the megawatt class Alpha laser, the four-meter LAMP primary mirror, and beam alignment and control technologies. At this point the coordinated experiments of this complete high-energy laser beam are being conducted on the ground.

As the threat of strategic nuclear war diminishes, BMDO research in free electron laser and neutral particle beam technologies has been discontinued. At the same time, the military has shifted to working collaboratively with civilian businesses for nonmilitary applications. The research originally developed for SDI and BMDO is spinning off into commercial applications, and some of the technologies have even found their way into medical care and entertainment-related products.

Laser Defense and Weapons

Missile detection and deterrents, land mine detection, and other laser-related military projects include a laser satellite communications system, which is being considered for implementation by both the U.S. Air Force and the Airborne Reconnaissance Office.

THEL

The Tactical High Energy Laser (THEL) is being developed by the U.S. Army Space and Missile Defense Command. Also known as the Nautilus laser system, THEL was first designed and built by Israel in 1996 and was later funded by the United States. In 2004, $56 million was allocated for research and development of the Nautilus Anti-Rocket System at White Sands Missile Range in New Mexico. The firm of Northrop Grumman in the United States was also involved. In 2006 Northrop Grummond announced the Sky-

Guard system, capable of tracking, deflecting, and destroying rocket, artillery, and mortar attacks.

Tests in July 2007 were successful, and a model of THEL tracked and shot down mortars and missiles, as well as targeting and destroying standing targets. The THEL model is capable of using an infrared beam to lock onto the target and update its trajectory during flight to track and intercept the attacker or a new target, such as a moving tank. A video of the test is available, at www.israelweapons.com, in which you can observe the laser unit tracking and destroying hand-launched mortars, larger missiles, and standing targets.

THEL is being developed to respond to "theater threats"— attacks by short-range rockets and artillery, cruise missiles, and pop-up helicopters that attack quickly and without much warning. The speed-of-light response of a laser is considered to be the best available way to effectively react to such sudden attacks.

New and/or in-work laser weapons include:

1. Skyguard
2. Airborne laser
3. Advanced tactical laser
4. High Energy Liquid Laser Area Defense System (HELLADS)

Land Mine Location and Laser-Induced Breakdown Spectroscopy (LIBS)

The presence of land mines has always been of great concern to the branches of the armed services that deploy ground troops. The army, navy, and marine corps are coordinating efforts to use advanced technology to detect these mines.

In 2005, two men, Robert W. Haupt and Kenneth D. Rolt, announced in the *Lincoln Laboratory Journal* (Vol. 15, No. 1, 2005) at MIT their study of a mine-detector that could be mounted on a truck and would use a directed narrow-beam parametric acoustic array (PAA) sound source and a laser Doppler vibrometer seismic detector. The operator could work from a safe distance, and the sound source would penetrate the ground, effectively making the mine vibrate. The laser vibrometer would then measure the vibrations of the ground to determine the type of object that was being detected. This experiment worked, but because of low signal force and other subtle weaknesses, it was not completely reliable. For more information on this standoff acoustic laser technique, go to www.mit.edu/news/journal/detector, for the complete journal publication and article.

Shortly after the MIT publication, Ning Xiang and J. M. Sabatier published in IEEE's *Geoscience and Remote Sensing Letters* the use of binary maximum-length sequences as the acoustic excitation for getting stronger scanning results, as well as some additional issues regarding system design and field results, which further improved upon Haupt and Rolt's technique to locate buried land mines.

The U.S. Army Research Laboratory and Ocean Optics are working together on a LIBS-based field system that can be carried in a backpack for measuring potentially hazardous objects and materials. The laser is in a handheld probe that has a microplasma tip. The operator can make effective evaluations of objects quickly in the field.

Jobs in Military Programs

Working with lasers as a member of the U.S. Armed Forces is another way in which men and women can find careers in laser technology. The first step in joining the armed forces is to talk with a recruiter. Your high school or career center counselor can put you in touch. Or you can check your local telephone book for listings. You can sign up at age seventeen with parental consent or at age eighteen without it. In peacetime, most young men and women who are enlisting have a high school diploma, and you'll need a personal record that is good enough to stand a thorough background check. In wartime, some of these restrictions are relaxed to a degree or waived altogether.

You'll be given the Armed Forces Qualifications Test, as well as the Armed Services Vocational Aptitude Battery. Your scores on those tests and your personal interests will determine what career paths are open to you, as will the particular needs of the service to which you are applying.

When you see a career counselor at the military entrance processing station, he or she will check your scores and show you a computer screen. On the first screen you see will be the categories the service really needs to recruit people for—at the highest level for which you qualify. The computer is updated daily to reflect current needs.

If you are joining the army, you might see a screen about a job classification with duties involving intermediate-level maintenance and repair on special electronic devices, such as mine detectors, battlefield illumination systems, warning systems, and various sensors. Although you will undoubtedly work with equipment other than lasers, laser technology will probably be involved in some of the sensing mechanisms. Training required for categories such as tank systems mechanic, armament and fire control maintenance supervisor, or topographic instrument repair specialist will also probably include working with laser technology.

Measurements in Space

Using lasers to measure distances in space has helped scientists learn more about the universe. Complicated mathematical models of how the universe acts have been devised, and extremely precise laser measurements help calculate "real" ranges. By comparing the predicted distances with those that have actually been measured, the Earth's orientation can thus be monitored. The International Laser Ranging Service (ILRS) maintains research stations in countries all over the world. Because the number of permanent lunar laser ranging stations around the globe is increasing (stations currently exist in North America, Europe, Eastern Europe, the Middle East, the Mediterranean, China, Russia, Australia, Tahiti, Hawaii, and South Africa), scientists can observe the surface of the entire Earth for plate tectonic motions that will help them in predicting earthquakes. Data from these ranging stations also help to determine tidal effects and changes in the Earth's rotation. Go to the website at www.ilrs.gsfc.nasa.gov for additional information about the work of the ILRS. You can also write to the service at the following address:

International Laser Ranging Service
Central Bureau NASA
Goddard Space Flight Center, Code 920.1
Greenbelt, Maryland 20771

In the late 1950s a group of physicists at Princeton University suggested using powerful pulsed searchlights on Earth to illuminate mirrors placed on satellites in orbit. By photographing a satellite's position with respect to the fixed background of stars, they hoped to analyze the characteristics of the satellite's motion while in orbit.

Once lasers had been invented, however, the scientists' plans changed. Because laser light has a precise wavelength, and because laser light can be produced in incredibly short pulses, measurements in space can now be made with a degree of precision and accuracy that was not even imagined earlier.

Lasers on the Moon

In 1969, as part of their Moon mission, Apollo 11 astronauts placed special reflectors on the Moon's surface. Later, scientists from McDonald Observatory at the University of Texas at Austin aimed pulses of light from a ruby laser at these reflectors. The length of time it took the laser pulses to hit the reflectors and return was measured extremely carefully. Then scientists calculated the distance to the moon (238,857 miles between the center of the Earth and the center of the Moon). Because the electronic circuits that measured the time were so sensitive, scientists believe that the distance to the moon has been accurately measured to within two to three meters.

Employment with NASA

Finding employment as a laser technician or scientist in the space program or in related fields will most likely require an advanced degree. However, if working in this field interests you as a student, you can contact university researchers, such as those at the University of Texas at Austin, or you can contact NASA directly.

NASA Student Programs

NASA has multiple locations in various parts of the country. If you go to the website at www.nasa.gov, you will find many informative features about NASA and its work. Clicking on the specific buttons will give you access to such sections as "Career Resources," "Research Opportunities," and "Astronaut Selection." You will also find special pages for students, with information on co-op work/study programs, as well as summer and internship programs. For these programs, you can access the website www.science.nasa .gov/about/students, and you will receive more information and instructions on how to apply. You can also subscribe to e-mail lists for announcements and bulletins, publications, and news releases about developments. You may be able to use the information you get from reading the releases to contact some of the scientists mentioned directly. Sometimes an individual scientist is willing to correspond with a young person, offering advice and suggestions.

If you are already a college student, or if you have completed a degree and know that you want to go into aeronautics or space research, you might write to the specific NASA location in which you are interested, for example, NASA Ames Research Center, Moffett Field, California 94035.

Other Military and Defense Employment

Many other areas of the United States government handle projects and work in cooperation with the United States Armed Forces. To research the broad scope of related jobs, go to www.usajobs.gov, which is the official job site of the United States government. On this website, you will find information about federal jobs and employment requirements by clicking on "Search Jobs," "Create Résumé," and other helpful sections that are presented there. Ample additional resources are also included.

6

LASERS IN COMMUNICATIONS

IF YOU THINK that handling twenty billion bits of data per second (bps) is fast, that impression will soon be topped, according to David Orenstein in an article published recently by Stanford University on the website www.physorg.com. Better and faster things are coming our way—and soon.

Ever-Faster Transmission

Orenstein notes that a telecommunications industry goal has been the transfer of data at forty billion bits per second, and he has a surprise. Announced in the October 31, 2007, edition of the journal *Optics Express* is a very special accomplishment by two scientists at Stanford. Assistant professor of electrical engineering Jelena Vuckovic and doctoral student Hatice Altug have reported a new type of solid-state laser that can do much better than that. With a single-mode laser that can be turned on and off and is more efficient, Vuckovic says that theoretically their photonic crystal laser will do more than one hundred billion bps. And there's more—they can also build lasers that will operate at different wavelengths and can send more than one wavelength of light at the same time, with each carrying its own stream of data.

This could be another major leap forward in an industry that has already surpassed all records for giant steps.

Until only recently, telecommunications was primarily electronic. In the 1960s and 1970s, the development of silica glass fibers made it possible to use light waves to transmit large amounts of information over long distances. In the 1980s, optical fiber systems increased the capacity and speed of transmission.

By the beginning of the twenty-first century, telecommunications had begun to rely on photons. Light traveling as photons, or tiny packets of radiant energy, can move extremely quickly, allowing various forms of communications—text, sound, images, data—to be routinely transported over huge distances. This process uses semiconductor lasers, which transmit the light pulses carrying billions of bits of information per second over hair-thin glass fibers.

The use of photons to transmit information is the basis of the field of photonics, which in its broadest definition includes all the elements of optical communications. The business of photonics is booming. Indeed, the amazing developments taking place at major research facilities are occurring so fast and furiously that groundbreaking discoveries are almost out of date before they have even fully entered the marketplace.

The increased role of the Internet and a growing demand for optical technology in storage, imaging, and switching means that this field will continue to expand in the future. Although the era of photonics began only in the 1980s, by 2007 photonics-related investments totaled more than $12 billion. Whether you would like to work in a large research facility or at a smaller company, the opportunities for employment in this field are very promising, as there are now several thousand photonics- and optics-related companies in the United States, many of them operating in the field of communications.

Role of Bell Laboratories

Begun in 1925 as a research and development company of the Bell System, Bell Labs was an AT&T subsidiary owned jointly by AT&T and Western Electric. In 1996, it became a part of the now defunct Lucent Technologies and is now a division of the new corporation Alcatel-Lucent. Since its beginning in 1926, Bell Labs has earned more than thirty-one thousand patents, with development of the LED and the discovery of the measurement of sound among them.

Thousands of people work for Bell Labs in such areas as microelectronics and digital signal processing, software and information sciences, optical networking technologies, wireless and photonics, image and speech processing, distributed computing, and Internet and access technologies.

Bell Labs has played a critical role in the history of the laser. It was 1960 when Ali Javan and his coworkers at the Bell Telephone Laboratories first operated the helium-neon gas discharge laser, only a few months after Ted Maiman had created the first working laser at Hughes Research Laboratories. Bell Labs scientist Arthur Schawlow (who in 1981 was to share a Nobel Prize for his work in laser spectroscopy) and his brother-in-law Charles Townes (a Nobel winner in 1964 for his work with the ammonia maser), were awarded a significant patent in 1960—a patent that they subsequently licensed to laser manufacturers.

By 1961, Bell Labs had developed the continuous-wave solid-state laser (neodymiumdoped calcium tungstate). A significant advance in light transmission of information came in 1970, when Bell Labs scientists developed a tiny solid-state laser capable of emitting usable amounts of concentrated light continuously at room temperature. By 1977, AT&T had installed the world's first light-wave system to carry voice, video, and data communications traffic in Chicago.

The developments in laser research continued apace at Bell Labs both in the years before and after the Bell research community became a part of Lucent Technologies. In more recent years, researchers at Bell Labs (in collaboration with scientists at Yale University and the Max Planck Institute of Physics in Germany) have worked on novel semiconductor microlasers that use "bow ties" of laser light to emit highly directional beams with more than a thousand times the power of conventional, disk-shaped microlasers. These microlasers are so small that hundreds could fit on the head of a pin.

Scientists at Bell Labs also discovered a way to make one laser do the work of 206 lasers. Using a single laser to generate light pulses (each lasting merely one hundred millionth of a billionth of a second), data were transmitted over 206 wavelengths, or colors, of light. (When data are transmitted, they are in the ones and zeros of digital information.) This transmission was the largest number of channels of communication ever generated.

In March 1999, at the one hundredth anniversary meeting of the American Physical Society, scientists from Bell Labs unveiled the world's highest-power mid-infrared semiconductor laser. This new, experimental quantum-cascade (QC) laser had more than a thousand times the output of any commercial semiconductor currently operating in the mid-infrared wavelength region.

Based on quantum physics and atomic layer control of semiconductor structures, the QC laser could be operated at room temperature, so it was more affordable than other semiconductor lasers. QC lasers operate like an electronic waterfall. The electrons cascade down an energy "staircase." Along the way, as they hit each "step," they produce photons (light pulses). Earlier QC lasers had twenty or thirty steps for the electrons to cascade down; in the newer version, electrons moved down seventy-five steps. The QC lasers, which were invented by scientists at Bell Labs, were developed for commercial use in areas such as collision avoidance, pollution monitoring, and medicine.

Optical Networking

By the mid-1990s, the phenomenal growth in the areas of Internet access and high-speed data transfer required Internet service providers (ISPs) to increase their fiber optic network capacity. It was possible to increase capacity by adding more fiber lines or by increasing terminal speeds with newer multiplexing systems. By the end of the decade, however, it had become clear that faster and more economical technologies were needed in order to meet the additional demands. For that reason, Bell Labs and other research facilities dedicated tremendous resources to developing optical networking systems, by which beams of light could be used to transmit information directly through the air.

In 1995, technology developed at Bell Labs came together in the first optical-networking system to use dense wave division multiplexing (DWDM) technology. This technology is used to expand the capacity of fiber-optic networks. Three years later, Lucent Technologies rolled out an optical networking system developed by Bell Labs that was capable of delivering up to four-hundred gigabits (billion bits) per second of information over a single strand of fiber. This immense amount of information is roughly the equivalent of transporting the traffic of the entire Internet at any given second over one fiber.

Another breakthrough optical networking system developed at Bell Labs was Lucent's WaveStar OpticAir system. This system used beams of light to transmit information directly through the air using lasers, amplifiers, and receivers that could be placed on rooftops or in office windows. The earliest applications of this wireless technology transformed communications in metropolitan areas and in campus environments worldwide—and in places where geography or other constraints made fiber connections harder to establish.

Lasers and Optical Storage

Lasers play an important role in compact disc (CD) and digital versatile disc (DVD) technology. Since their introduction, audio compact disc players, CDs, and DVDs have become "must-haves" in every American home, car, and office.

The disc has billions of microscopic pits on its aluminum surface. In these pits, music is stored in digital form. During playback, a laser beam scans the pits as the disc is spinning inside the player, sending the information from the pits to a computer chip, which converts it into sound.

Optical data storage provides tremendous advantages of capacity. An optical disc that's smaller than the older computer floppy can store the equivalent of a quarter of a million pages of typed information.

Originally, optical discs had read-only memory (ROM). Eventually, companies developed erasable-disc technology. In May 1988, Tandy Corporation announced plans to license rights to the dye-polymer technology, which uses a high-intensity laser beam to encode a disc that is especially coated and a lower-power laser beam to read back the information. Hitachi and Sony also worked on similar technology. Research and development experts in other corporations have developed erasable disks for computers that are based on a technology that uses a laser for changing magnetic properties.

Today's optical disc technology is speeding computer operations. Banks and investment firms using optical discs find that data from multiple workstations in its own building, across the country, or even on the other side of the world are quickly accessible.

For instance, when a customer comes in to apply for a loan, the person taking the information can tap into the bank's mainframe database and use its information to help assess the creditworthiness of the applicant. Credit histories, credit checks, and other documents relating to that customer may be scattered throughout bank files, in branches in another city, or perhaps in Europe. Optical disc storage and retrieval, however, lets the loan officer access the information randomly and quickly.

Professional Working Conditions

What does the revolutionary speed of this technology mean to you or to anyone who wants to work with laser technology in the communications, financial, or related areas that use this technology primarily for data transmission?

If you want to work in this fast-paced, competitive environment, you must keep up with developments. You will need to know the communications needs of different kinds of organizations and also the latest technology developments—as they occur—to help meet those needs. Working in this part of the industry requires a particularly strong involvement in lifelong education.

You will need continually to observe the developing technology and to learn new software and new applications of new kinds of lasers as they come along. You will want to know which companies and research centers are the strongest and the most important to watch. It will be important to follow the financial health of the major communications companies, so read major technology and communications trade journals and general business news magazines such as *Time*, *Business Week*, *Fortune*, and *Forbes* on the Internet or in paper copies.

You will find helpful information in computer and Internet magazines, as well. Check the Internet or your public library for the *Wall Street Journal*. Read reports, analyses, and forecasts. Many companies maintain elaborate websites, such as AT&T's site at www.att.com. Most of the corporations and other organizations will maintain a website feature labeled "Employment," "Careers," or "Job Search." Check their needs, and think through the requirements that they list. Because of intense competition among the companies, skills in sales and marketing will be important tools as you look for jobs—along with proven ability to understand the technology and work with it.

Lasers and the Revolution in Printing

Dave Packard and Bill Hewlett started their company in 1939 in a garage behind the Packards' home in Palo Alto, California, with $583 in capital. It has grown to one of the top corporations in America.

Although HP makes more than ten thousand products, one of the best-known is its desktop laser printer. The LaserJet printers work well with more than six hundred of the most popular computer software programs. Introduced in 1984, when the company "broke the barrier of the $100,000 laser printer" by inventing the desktop LaserJet for under $5,000, the printers have been runaway bestsellers. Small versions today are well within a middle-class family's budget, and more corporations and individuals own LaserJet printers than all other laser printers combined.

"A laser printer is based on copier technology," explained Jeri Peterson, press coordinator at Hewlett-Packard Boise Printer Operation. "There's an internal laser in the printer. When you type information into your PC via a software package, that data is transferred to the printer. It controls where the laser beam writes by exposing an area on a round photosensitive drum.

"Laser printers put the power of professional printing into everybody's hands; they're quiet, flexible, and fast. Because they're not tied to a font ball, like a daisywheel printer, users have the ability to integrate text and graphics—in fact, to do high-quality desktop publishing with a broad variety of well-developed software programs—in their storefront office, for their church or mosque or synagogue newsletter, or their high school yearbook. The printing industry has changed drastically because of this technology, and more and more printing is being done on-site in offices and homes, rather than being sent out to offsite printers."

One Press Relations Coordinator's Career

Peterson didn't expect to be handling press relations for HP's Boise printer operation when she finished two years at a junior college in Washington State. In fact, she wasn't sure just what she wanted to do, so she tried several jobs. She was a nanny for a California family, a hospital phlebotomist in a medical lab, an au pair in Paris where she worked for her room and board while taking French classes, and eventually a college student again when she realized that she needed a degree.

Earning her bachelor's degree in fine arts from the University of Washington, Seattle, she signed up for a campus recruitment interview. HP was looking for an industrial designer, but they hired Peterson as a graphic designer in the disk memory division that made large disk drives for HP's minicomputer systems. By 1984, when HP introduced the new LaserJet technology to dealers, a new system of marketing was needed, and Peterson was on the ground floor. HP used a "Dealer Channel" group as support for dealers. Peterson supported the eastern region, doing dealer presentations. She wrote proposals and documentation for desktop publishing applications.

By March 1987, when HP introduced the LaserJet Series II, the company was essentially making two earlier models obsolete. New, effective sales promotion for their dealers was needed immediately if HP was to meet its goal of adding unit sales to make up for rolling over the higher-priced models. A time crunch came up, and Peterson found herself coordinating fourteen separate promotion projects.

Several years later, now based in Boise, Idaho, Peterson dealt mainly with the computer trade press. She was responsible for talking with editors when they phoned in, finding out what they needed, and setting up interviews with on-site management people. Surveys showed that PC-oriented consumer publications and trade press reviews played an important role in the user's buying decision, so the impact of successful public relations was strong.

Since HP had flexible hours, Peterson picked her own starting time, generally choosing to begin work at 6:00 A.M. If editors were visiting, she dressed more formally; otherwise casual dress was fine, she said. One day found her awaiting an editor who wanted to write about HP's technical service phone line and who wanted to interview the college students who worked part-time taking as many as twenty thousand phone calls a month from HP customers. Before the editor arrived, Peterson had briefed the call center's manager on the kinds of questions the editor might ask and how to handle sensitive issues. After a ninety-minute meeting with the manager, she made sure all was ready for the continental breakfast she'd planned.

Peterson sat in on the interviews—not to censor them, because she generally didn't even talk during them, but to make sure that the HP manager covered key issues.

All went smoothly, but Peterson also sat in when the editor spent an hour with a student who was manning the lines. By the time she returned to her desk, she found ten pink slips—phone calls from editors of other publications and from market analysts. Although she was not the HP spokesperson on strategic issues, Peterson spent time talking with her managers, getting them to return calls. She briefed them on who the editor was, so that when an article appeared, the HP message would be there and would come across clearly.

Another important component of Peterson's job was responsibility for product-introduction public relations. HP used a Los Angeles–based agency for writing news releases; Peterson coordinated with the agency, often traveling there to discuss sales promotion and press ideas. With 40 percent of her time spent on phone calls and 20 percent in travel, Peterson had a long workday. She tried to leave by 6:00 P.M., and she had a computer and LaserJet printer at home. She often worked weekends at home and generally did not come into the office. Her short-term goal: to free up time to do more product introduction planning.

Salary for a job in an in-house public relations position can range from $45,000 to $120,000. Jobs at outside public relations firms often pay far more because agencies with high-tech clients need very qualified public relations professionals. Although she did not have an M.B.A., she recommends that degree for anyone who wants to be involved in the business side of laser products. Her advice to young people starting out: "Don't be afraid to try things, even if they're outside your area of expertise. Stretch and risk a little in what you are doing."

Sales, marketing, public relations, dealer relations, promotion, and publicity are all nontechnical areas, but they are involved with ideas and many company areas in which people wanting work involving lasers can find enjoyment and satisfying careers.

Holograms

Dennis Gabor, the "father of holography," coined the terms *hologram* and *holography* in 1947. The word *hologram* comes from the Greek words *holos*, meaning whole or complete, and *gram*, meaning message.

Holograms have been described as painting with light. That's not strictly true, of course, but to people who watched Dr. Tung H. Jeong, Albert Blake Dick Professor of physics at Lake Forest (Illinois) College and author of *Laser Holography: Experiments You Can Do*, it seems as if that was what he was doing. Magically, through using a simple laser and everyday objects, Jeong demonstrated that laser light could make a color picture on black-and-white film, without a camera—a picture that could be seen with ordinary light.

The process looked simple. Yet, Jeong said, four separate Nobel Prizes had been awarded for the theories contained in that one sentence. In order to make the process easier to understand, Jeong used what he called the "soap bubble theory." He showed children how, with just water from the sink, it's possible to produce beautiful soap bubbles with all the colors of the rainbow. It's the same theory, he says, that lies behind how we get holograms in color from black-and-white film.

How Lasers Make Holograms

When Jeong made a hologram, he split the laser beam in two with a lens. One of the two beams bounced off the object Jeong was using and was reflected back onto photographic film. The other beam from the laser hit the film directly but did not bounce off the subject. Although both halves of the beam were coherent when they left the laser, they were no longer coherent when they reached the film. Some of the light waves that struck the film arrived in certain patterns, producing a double-strength wave called a *reinforcement*. Other waves showed a pattern producing a *cancellation*. These patterns were recorded on the film. The resulting hologram could be used to reconstruct a three-dimensional picture of the object.

One of the most fascinating things about holograms is that you can cut up one of them into tiny pieces. Yet, if you look closely, you will see that, unlike ordinary photographs, each small fragment contains a full representation of the complete object.

How Holograms Are Used

If you look at almost any credit card, you will probably see that it contains a hologram. If you see a multicolored three-dimensional image of the MasterCard or Visa logo, you have a transmission hologram. Another common use of holograms, though you may not realize it, often happens at the supermarket checkout counter.

The clerk passes one of your items over the scanner window. A spinning hologram under the counter locates the bar code on the product. The hologram directs the reflected light back from the bar code into the store's computer, which has been programmed to recognize the item and to enter its price on the cash register.

Corporations also use holograms as an attention-getter. Jeong himself was commissioned to photograph former Olympic gymnast Mary Lou Retton for possible use of the hologram by McDonald's, one of her sponsors. "We went to Salt Lake City for the project," Jeong recalled, "since I had a friend there with some special equipment." Retton was photographed with a light exposure of one twentieth billionth of a second with a special lens, and under vibration-free conditions. Jeong created a similar photograph of Ronald McDonald for use in McDonald's annual franchise show at Las Vegas.

Holograms have many other uses. One that might not occur to you can be thought of as being similar to time-lapse photography. As Jeong reported at a meeting of the International Society of Optical Engineers, "Once you've made a hologram, you can compare what you recorded with the living and growing object. For instance, you can superimpose a hologram image of a mushroom on top of the growing fungus. You can measure the growth, second by second, as it grows in real-time—as you watch the differences between the static hologram and the living fungus."

This ability to compare recorded versus actual objects makes using holograms helpful in nondestructive testing. An aircraft tire can be recorded on a hologram and then inflated. If there is a defect in the tire, that area will expand at a slightly larger rate than the rest of the tire. The trouble spot shows up when compared to the baseline hologram.

Holograms can even show antimatter. Working with Jeong, scientists at Fermilab near Batavia, Illinois, recorded bubbles formed in a liquefied hydrogen chamber—particles that existed for only ten to twelve seconds. The bubbles that formed for such a brief time could be photographed by laser light.

Information storage is another technology that Jeong and other researchers were pioneering. One of his friends from China was able to record entire encyclopedias on a single sheet of film—pages that could be randomly accessed. With such a technology, it would be possible to store your entire personal medical record on a piece of plastic the size of a credit card.

Another application for holograms has been to record cultural items. Treasures from the Soviet Union and from the ancient civilization of Thrace were photographed with laser light, and their resulting holograms were sold as art objects. It was Soviet scientists, in fact, who worked out the process by which holograms are made so that they are visible under normal white light; a second kind of hologram, invented earlier, could be viewed only by laser light.

One Holography Artist's Career

Doris Vila, chair of the Department of Holography at the School of the Art Institute of Chicago, was herself an accomplished holographer. One of her commissioned holographic works was at the School of Nursing, University of Wisconsin–Eau Claire.

Vila, who said that she began holography from the artistic rather than the scientific side, became interested in the subject even before she saw her first hologram in 1979. She wanted to know more, and eventually she viewed holography as a fine art form rather than just a revolution in imaging technology.

She explained holograms to students by asking them to imagine that they are "standing at the edge of a pond, throwing in a stone that generates wavelets out in circles. When you throw in a second stone, it too has circles of wavelets. At a certain point where wave crests generated from each stone meet—where crest meets crest—it gets higher, and where crest and trough meet, they cancel each other out. Imagine that we can make a small metal grating that captures the interference pattern. We'd insert it into the pond and let everything go still again. Yet the grating would record those patterns."

Holography Education

In most art schools, courses are offered in beginning and in intermediate/advanced holography, sometimes as a part of the digital art program and sometimes as a part of an optics program. There may also be other names. The beginning course may be a full semester of hands-on learning, in which students set up their own cameras, tune spatial filters, and work with their own personal imagery. Although the emphasis is on artistic results, students study the structure of light, as well as the theory and techniques of three-dimensional imaging. If they wish, students can sign up for additional hours of working time in the lab each week.

Advanced students gain a working knowledge of multi-image display holograms, as well as techniques for producing master holograms, both for white light transmission and reflection work. Students in an M.F.A. program can also emphasize holography in their studies.

Not all schools offer courses in holography, but most large colleges and universities do, often in the college of optical sciences, the department of physics, or the department of communications technology, in addition to (or instead of) the department of art. A brief list of some of these schools follows. You can visit their websites for more information and/or to request catalogs. Major schools in China, England, France, Germany, India, Italy, Japan, Korea, Russia, and other countries offer courses, as well.

- Carnegie Mellon University
- Illinois Institute of Technology
- Indiana State University
- Kettering University
- Lake Forest College
- Massachusetts Institute of Technology
- New York University
- Ohio State University
- Pratt Institute of Design
- School of the Art Institute of Chicago
- University of Arizona
- University of California–Los Angeles
- University of Florida
- University of Maryland
- University of Massachusetts
- University of Oklahoma
- University of Texas
- University of Toronto
- University of Wisconsin
- Washington State University

7

LASERS IN RESEARCH

MANY RESEARCH SCIENTISTS work in academic, scientific, and government facilities to discover new laser technologies and their uses. For others, there is a very strong link between their laser research and its commercial applications. For example, the research facilities of Bell Labs are key sites of laser research. While most of the developments have a strong relevance to immediate commercial enterprise, other areas of Bell Labs are engaged in long-range research that is less immediately commercial.

Technology Transfer

Technology transfer—to and from military and space programs—is taking place in a number of locations, including the various military service research and development agencies, NASA centers, and federal laboratories. Here, significant advances in technology and recent inventions from military programs are being studied. Scientists hope they will be able to use them commercially. Many of these items are already being produced by the private sector, and others will become the new products of tomorrow.

The laser technology involved in the Strategic Defense Initiative (SDI) created a broad range of spin-offs, which can add up to significant benefits in terms of human welfare, industrial efficiency, and economic value.

Qualified American business and academic clients who have been approved under procedures established by the Department of Defense can learn about civil applications of military technology through a referral database. Open to all federal and state agencies, the database is accessible through a computer modem. Technology application panels were established in various areas, including biomedical applications; electronics, communications, and computer applications; power-generation, storage, and transmission applications; and materials and industrial process applications.

Medical Free-Electron Laser Program

Since 1985 Congress has funded medical, biomedical, and materials research on free-electron laser technology. Regional medical free-electron laser research centers have been established at a number of facilities.

In addition, preclinical medical research on surgical applications, therapy, and the diagnosis of disease is being conducted at, among other locations, the Massachusetts General Hospital, the University of Utah, Northwestern University, Baylor Medical School, and the University of California at Irvine. Biophysics research is being carried out at, for example, the University of Michigan, Purdue University, the University of Texas, and Jackson Laboratories (Maine). Materials science is being investigated at Brown University, the State University of New York at Buffalo, the University of Utah, Stanford, Vanderbilt, Princeton, Southern Methodist, and other universities and research centers.

Other Spin-Off Applications

Key examples of SDI technology that have found potential civil applications provide a substantial economic return on investment. They include optical computing, using laser light instead of electrical circuits for transmitting data; more efficient, less expensive electrical power systems; lightweight mirrors that can be aligned through computer control and used for lasers in manufacturing processes; and integration of laser technology, robotics, and computerized techniques for precision control into applications for manufacturing processes and biomedical work.

In addition, free-electron lasers have been used in noninvasive cancer surgery, in the early diagnosis and treatment of heart disease and stroke, and in other medical diagnostic and treatment applications and procedures.

Scientists in the laboratories mentioned above are working hard at finding new and practical uses for lasers. You can learn more about what they are doing by visiting their websites, writing to the public relations offices of the universities and hospitals, and asking to be put on the mailing list for copies of news releases mentioning lasers.

Laser Fusion

Research into laser fusion offers another career opportunity for working with lasers. If laser fusion energy can be commercially feasible, it could provide an environmentally safe form of energy that is virtually inexhaustible.

The sun generates its energy through thermonuclear fusion of hydrogen atoms. Fusion energy research on Earth is an effort to re-create and harness that energy. In the sun, gravity holds charged particles together in a tightly packed mass. That's why fusion reactions can occur on the sun at temperatures of about fourteen million degrees. But because Earth has only a fraction of the sun's enormous gravity, scientists must create more extreme conditions to make fusion possible.

On Earth the fuel density of a fusion reaction must be in the range of ten to twenty times that of lead, and temperatures must reach about fifty million degrees. When these conditions have been achieved, the fusion fuel undergoes a thermonuclear "burn." As a result, large amounts of energy are released—many times more energy than the laser beam emitted to start the reaction.

At the University of Rochester in 1988, the Laboratory for Laser Energetics used a twelve-trillion watt OMEGA laser system to study the potential of high-powered lasers to produce controlled thermonuclear fusion. To do this, target pellets of fusion fuel had to be heated and compressed so rapidly that the fusion fuel would burn before the highly compressed hot material flew apart. Powerful laser beams—split, amplified, and converted from infrared light to ultraviolet (which is more effectively absorbed by the target pellets)—were focused precisely on the pellets. When the beams hit the pellets, the surface matter blasted outward at a velocity of nearly six hundred miles per second. An equal force imploded on the shell containing the fuel.

The OMEGA laser was the size of a football field. The beams it emitted arrived at the target within a millionth of a millionth of a second of one another at a spot defined by dimensions smaller than a tenth of the diameter of a human hair.

Scientists at Rochester achieved a major milestone when they used the OMEGA laser to compress and heat a small capsule of fusion fuel to the highest density achieved that had ever been directly measured—in the range of two to four times that of lead, with a temperature in the range of five to ten million degrees. The fusion fuel was compressed to a density more than one hundred times its normal liquid density. If you could compress water to the same degree, an eight-ounce glass would weigh about fifty pounds. A gallon of water, compressed to the same degree as the fusion fuel in the laser experiments, would weigh nearly half a ton.

Sophisticated technology allowed the scientists to split each of OMEGA's twenty-four laser beams into several thousand beams that struck the target simultaneously. The target pellets were glass shells about the size of a grain of sand containing a frozen layer of fusion fuel. To compress the pellets evenly and prevent an area on their surface from "ballooning out," the laser had to irradiate the entire surface of the spherical fuel pellets with a high degree of uniformity. Splitting the beams so they struck the fuel pellets simultaneously let the laser do this.

The burst of energy from the OMEGA laser that compressed and heated the fusion fuel was incredibly short. The blast of laser light lasted about six-tenths of a nanosecond (six-tenths of a billionth of a second). For that period of time the OMEGA laser was twenty times brighter than the peak generating capacity of all the electrical generating plants in the United States.

Additional research in laser fusion is being conducted at other laboratories in the United States and Canada, including the Lawrence Livermore National Laboratory in Livermore, California. Scientists there are using the extremely large Nova laser for similar inertial confinement experiments.

Laser Isotope Separation

Scientists at the Lawrence Livermore National Laboratory also used lasers to separate isotopes to increase the concentration of valuable forms of the elements uranium and plutonium. Their goal was to help keep the price of American enriched uranium competitive with the price charged by foreign companies.

In its natural state, uranium is a mixture of two isotopes: U-235 and U-238. But U-235 amounts to only about 0.7 percent of natural uranium by weight. Uranium used as fuel in a nuclear reactor must have 3 percent of U-235. Consequently, natural uranium must be enriched.

Because different uranium isotopes absorb light tuned to different wavelengths, laser light—precisely tuned to desired wavelengths—separates the isotopes. The system used two types of lasers: dye lasers to generate the light used for photoionization of the uranium and copper-vapor lasers to energize the dye lasers. Powerful green-yellow light from copper-vapor lasers was converted to red-orange light in the dye laser. This red-orange light was tuned to the precise colors that are absorbed by U-235 but not by U-238.

In the Livermore project, uranium was heated in a vacuum chamber. A set of laser beams, tuned to wavelengths that match those of the desired U-235 atoms, passed through the vapor. When the atoms absorbed the laser light, they picked up enough energy to give up one of their negatively charged electrons. The U-235 atoms—now positively charged—were pulled from the vapor by an electric field and became enriched uranium, which could be made into fuel to drive nuclear power reactors. The U-238 atoms, which don't have an electrical charge, passed through the electric field and onto a collector.

Laser Research at Battelle

At Battelle Memorial Institute, numerous scientists, engineers, economists, and supporting specialists conduct thousands of studies per year with an annual business volume of approximately a billion dollars. Much of this work is done by Battelle under contract from industrial organizations and government agencies.

Laser research at Battelle-Columbus is handled by a special laser technology group. In an assortment of programs, Battelle developed applications of high-powered CO_2 laser radiation for welding, cutting, transformation hardening, and cladding of metals; and lasers were studied for improvements in cutting, shaping, and thermal processing of glasses and ceramics.

Battelle scientists studied two types of Nd-doped lasers: an Nd:YAG laser, which is used for testing various industrial processes, and an Nd:glass laser.

Another laser project at Battelle focused on laser shock hardening. When a laser beam was shot into metal, it could make the metal sixty times stronger. One Battelle scientist received a patent, and metal companies worked with Battelle to commercialize the process.

Jobs in Research

Research scientists who work with lasers have challenging careers. On the one hand, they have the knowledge that puts them on the frontier of technology; on the other hand, funding for research and development projects is often dependent on outside sources, such as Congress or private companies. Consequently, how many jobs there will be and who will get (and keep) them may depend on how successful the laboratory is at coming up with proposals or landing contracts.

One way to learn about these jobs is by reading the trade publications. For instance, a postdoctoral position in ultrafast laser spectroscopy at Hampton University in Hampton, Virginia, was advertised in *Optics and Photonics News*, published by the Optical Society of America. This publication also carries employment listings for laser-related positions in the military and business, as well as for international academic and research positions.

To qualify for these and other positions, candidates should have a doctor's or a master's degree in physics, electrical engineering, or mechanical engineering. In addition, they should be experienced in such fields as quantum optics, atmospheric physics, optical engineering, image and signal processing, or circuit design.

Security Clearance

Security has received extra attention ever since the attacks on the World Trade Center towers in New York in 2001. Because many research laboratories are working on government-funded projects, U.S. citizenship is usually a requirement for employment. In addition, your personal record must meet requirements for obtaining security clearance. Laboratories are generally equal opportunity employers and welcome applications from qualified candidates, regardless of sex or minority background. Salaries are competitive, and benefits are generally comprehensive.

In labs like Battelle, entry-level jobs for laser technicians require a two-year program in technology. Typically, the technician runs the equipment. The next level up is that of laser researcher—a man or woman who often runs experiments as well as does day-to-day laser operations. Most researchers have a four-year degree; however, Battelle promoted one laser technician who attended Ohio State University (with tuition help from Battelle) and who received a bachelor's degree.

Next highest position? Project researcher, if you're managing projects. Generally, a master's degree is the prerequisite. Persons like Frank, who have a Ph.D., can become research scientists, who are basically in charge of medium-sized projects or handle a certain subsection of a major project.

Laser Research Scientist

One of the roles Frank finds himself playing is that of fund-raiser. "At Battelle, principal research scientists like me are essentially people who get ideas, think up projects, and then go out and try to find people to pay for them," he explains. "For instance, I have the CO_2 laser lab. In our laser paint-stripping research, we run tests, and then we try to find people who want to strip paint."

Frank's days usually start at 8:30 A.M. and end at 5:30 P.M., though in research labs, he says, the hours are somewhat flexible.

A typical day recently found Frank helping to host a visiting group from a tractor company interested in laser robotics. Though the group spent the entire day at Battelle, he spoke with them for about two hours, leading them on a tour of his part of the facilities. Two or three more hours that day were spent in writing proposals and in catching up with his correspondence. Later he helped troubleshoot in another lab, assisting the scientists there to solve problems on their project and arranging for equipment to be built for their future needs.

Although Battelle has no hard-and-fast rule, Frank says, roughly 40 percent of his time should be spent in marketing Battelle's services. That may involve travel to prospective companies that might fund projects or arranging for Battelle to do contract research with another company.

Salaries for scientists at his level, he says, range between $68,000 and $93,000—higher on the coasts because of the cost-of-living difference. Frank says that senior research scientists in laboratories might earn more than $100,000.

His advice to young people who want to work with laser research is to look for universities or hospitals with laboratories and get hired at the technician level. Ohio State University has a research foundation similar to Battelle's, he says, in which companies with a problem can hire a team headed by an OSU professor to work on it. Such a lab affiliated with a university is a good source of openings for laser technicians, Frank says. "It's a good way to start in the laser area."

Major Laser Research Centers

Laser research is being carried out in large and small laboratories in nearly every major city of the United States, in hospitals and medical centers, industrial and corporate laboratories, colleges and universities and medical schools, and in foundation and research institutes.

Some important research centers are presented in the list that follows. The professional societies and associations provided in Appendix A can steer you toward many more. And outstanding research centers can be found in the list of laser-research related colleges and universities listed in Appendix B.

- Advanced Laser Light Source, ALLS Project/Quebec, www.mcgill.ca
- Argonne National Laboratory, www.anl.gov
- Brookhaven National Laboratory, www.bnl.gov
- Center for Laser and Photonics Research, Oklahoma State University, www.osu-ours.okstate.edu
- CERN, the European Organization for Nuclear Research, the world's largest particle physics laboratory, on the border between France and Switzerland, www.cern.ch
- Colorado State University, Collaboration on Laser Research and Photonics in the State of Colorado; University of Colorado; and Colorado School of Mines, www.centers.colorado.edu
- CREOL College of Optics and Photonics at the University of Central Florida, www.creol.ucf.edu
- Fermi National Laboratory, www.fnal.gov
- Institute of Laser Technology, Headquarters, Munich; offices in the United States and many other countries, www.fraunhofer.de
- Hampton Roads Research Partnership, large consortium of seven universities and other research organizations, with

affiliations with government and other research organizations, www.hamptonroadsrp.org

- Huazhong University of Science and Technology, China; State Engineering Research Center of Laser Processing, Cooperates with CAS Shanghai Optical Machinery Institute, CAS Anhui Optical Machinery Institute, and China Measuring Science Research Institute, www.hust.edu
- Idaho National Laboratory, www.inel.gov
- Laser Research Center for Molecular Research, Japan; pioneering work with ultraviolet and infrared lasers, www.ims.ac.jp
- Lawrence Berkeley National Laboratory, www.lbl.gov
- Lawrence Livermore National Laboratory, www.llnl.gov
- Los Alamos National Laboratory, www.lanl.gov
- Massachusetts Institute of Technology, www.mit.edu
- National Ignition Facility Programs, www.nif.gov
- National Renewable Energy Laboratory, www.nrel.gov
- National Research Council of Canada, www.nrc.cnrc.gc.ca
- New Brunswick National Laboratory, www.nbl.gov
- Oak Ridge National Laboratory, www.ornl.gov
- Pacific North West National Laboratory, www.pnl.gov
- Palo Alto Research Center, Subsidiary of the Xerox Corporation, www.parc.com
- Princeton Plasma Physics National Laboratory, www.pppl.gov
- Radiology and Environmental National Laboratory, www.insl.gov
- Sandia National Laboratory, www.sandia.gov

- Stanford Linear Accelerator Laboratory,
  www.slac.stanford.edu
- Thomas Jefferson National Laboratory, www.jlab.org
- University of Arizona, College of Optical Sciences,
  www.optics.arizona.edu
- University of Toronto, www.utoronto.ca

8

Preparing for a Career in Laser Technology

With the tremendous expansion that has taken place in the applications and uses of lasers, the opportunities to work in a job that utilizes laser technology have never been greater.

Lasers have become an integral part of manufacturing, communications, energy research, medicine, and dozens of other fields. Careers in laser technology are arrived at by many paths, and you will most likely find your path by preparing for a career in a field that appeals to you on a number of levels. Perhaps you are drawn to the prospect of helping people recover from illnesses or accidents and will find a career working with lasers in health care, whether as a doctor, ophthalmologist's assistant, nurse, or laser technician. Or maybe you are happiest when working alone in a research setting and will be looking for employment in a university or commercial research laboratory. You might even find your place as a holographic or laser light show artist! Whatever route you take, be certain that the challenges of working with lasers require a strong mind for detail and a passion for learning new techniques, as laser technology is sure to be developing rapidly.

Science Literacy

Working in laser technology calls for a solid understanding of the mathematical and scientific principles at work in lasers. The more math and science competency you develop, the better equipped you will be when faced with the complex concepts of physics and optics involved in laser technology. You can even start preparing for your future in lasers while still in junior high school by taking any extra math and science classes that are offered at your school. Even though you may not be working in an area directly related to lasers, the additional scientific and mathematical training will serve you well in the future.

In fact, there is a great push in the United States to try and improve math and science literacy. A person who is science-literate is someone who understands that science, math, and technology are interdependent human enterprises, each with its own benefits and drawbacks. Science literacy also calls for an understanding of key concepts and principles of science, as well as a familiarity with the diversity and unity of the natural world. Finally, someone who is science literate uses scientific knowledge for his or her individual and social purposes.

In 1996, the American Association for the Advancement of Science (AAAS), the National Academy of Sciences, and the National Science Teachers Association released a joint statement announcing their commitment to science literacy for all Americans. The drive for greater science literacy began in 1985, when the AAAS began a long-term project aimed at changing the way that science, math, and technology were taught in schools in the United States. That same year, Halley's comet was in view. The panel of experts at the AAAS considered how many scientific and technological changes a child just beginning school in 1985 would see before Halley's comet returned in 2061. Would he or she be prepared to understand, contribute to, and benefit from the changes that lay ahead?

The experts, who included scientists, mathematicians, and technologists, decided to launch what they called Project 2061 to establish guidelines for science literacy. Project 2061 produced two significant reports: *Science for All Americans* (1990) and *Benchmarks for Science Literacy* (1993). These important reports challenged the established methods of teaching science by creating a coherent set of specific learning goals for elementary, middle, and high school students. These benchmarks were instrumental in shaping the National Science Education Standards, which are used by school districts throughout the United States to create science and mathematics curricula. The Project 2061 experts also determined the process of truly coming to understand that new concepts cannot be rushed and must be presented periodically in different settings and at increasingly sophisticated levels of difficulty.

As the process of fostering scientific literacy throughout the country moves forward, what can you do to ensure that you are well-trained in the basic principles? The most direct answer is to enroll in the widest range of science and math classes available.

If you think you want to work with lasers, you will need to collaborate closely with guidance counselors, math and science instructors, and other school personnel and benefit from every opportunity.

Although you will want to extend yourself in science and math, it is important not to neglect the other academic subjects. You will want to do well in English classes, as good spoken and written communication skills are crucial to your success, especially when you are called upon to write reports and make presentations. You will want to be proficient in using computers, as they are inextricably linked with laser technologies.

The Optical Society of America (OSA) a society of more than fourteen thousand scientists, engineers, and entrepreneurs in a wide array of disciplines and industries, many of whom work directly with lasers—has a number of educational options for students. The OSA offers a rich variety of resources on lasers. For more information, contact the Optical Society of America at www.osa.org.

College and Beyond

As lasers have moved into every corner of our lives, colleges and universities have developed specialized programs for undergraduate, graduate, postdoctoral, and continuing education in optical science and engineering and the many specialized applications of laser light.

Programs in optics are often offered within physics or electrical engineering departments at many universities, but some schools have established comprehensive programs offering degrees in optics as a separate discipline. Whether you obtain your college or graduate degree in optics from a physics department or from a separate optical sciences department, you will receive instruction from fundamental through applied science to engineering. If you study in a traditional science department such as physics, you will find that this discipline tends to stress the scientific aspect of optics rather than the applications. Should you study at a program that is part of an electrical engineering department, you will find the emphasis to be more on how the technology is applied.

The specialized optics programs are more likely to encompass fundamental and applied subjects equally. The faculty for the specialized programs is drawn from a variety of disciplines, including physics, engineering, and materials science. Most of these programs are designed for graduate study, so it will be necessary to get your undergraduate science degree first.

"If you want to do graduate study in optics and lasers, any good university with a good program in physics or electrical engineering can prepare you," said Dr. M. J. Soileau, of CREOL, the University of Central Florida's Center for Research and Education in Optics and Lasers.

He advised that, "You really need a solid background in either physics or applied physics. You need a very strong math background, starting with calculus. As a college undergraduate, take as much math as you can, at the highest level of sophistication possible. The more you're proficient in math, the easier it is to do the science and the engineering. A good background in physics and engineering—preferably electrical engineering—will help you if you want to do laser research."

University of Rochester

The Laboratory for Laser Energetics, a multidisciplinary teaching and research unit of the College of Engineering and Applied Science at the University of Rochester, was the first of its kind at any American college or university. Students are involved in all of the research programs, including a project to explore the potential of high-powered lasers to produce controlled thermonuclear fusion as an alternative energy source. The laboratory's principal research tool is a twelve-trillion-watt laser system, the world's most powerful UV laser. At the laboratory, research activities include major programs in photo-matter interactions, optical materials development, laser physics and technology, and the physics of ultrahigh density phenomena.

The laboratory contains the Ultrafast Science Center, which investigates the production and utilization of phenomena occurring on time scales of less than a billionth of a second.

Undergraduate students who want to concentrate in engineering are assigned faculty advisers in the College of Engineering and Applied Science in their freshman year. They may (and usually do) begin taking engineering courses as early as their first semester. During their first two years, they receive a strong liberal arts education. In the spring of their sophomore year students apply formally to the College of Engineering and Applied Science by filing a "concentration approval" form, in which they list an approved plan of study for their last two years.

A special five-year program is available for electrical engineering students who contemplate graduate work. Students are accepted into this program in the junior year and can begin master's-level independent work in the senior year. At the end of the five-year program, both bachelor's and master's degrees in electrical engineering are awarded.

Institute of Optics

The Institute of Optics at the University of Rochester is an internationally known center for teaching and research. The institute offers programs of study leading to the B.S., M.S., and Ph.D.

degrees in optics. Optics majors may apply in their junior year for admission to the five-year B.S., M.S. program. Students normally apply for admission to the Institute of Optics at the end of the sophomore year. Certain prerequisite courses and minimum grade point averages are required.

Qualified undergraduates often are able to take part in various faculty research projects. Programs in the Institute of Optics cover a fundamentals-to-applications continuum, including imaging, lasers, optical materials, optics manufacturing, semiconductor lasers, theoretical foundations, ultrafast phenomena, as well as diffractive-fiber, gradient-index, guided-wave, nonlinear, and quantum optics.

The Institute of Optics is home to the Laboratory for Laser Energetics, the Center for Electronic Imaging Systems, and the Center for Optics Manufacturing.

Prospective students and undergraduates considering optics as a major are encouraged to write to the Institute of Optics, University of Rochester, Rochester, New York 14627. Or they can visit its website at www.optics.rochester.edu to find out more.

University of Arizona

The University of Arizona, Tucson, Optical Sciences Center (OSC) is a graduate center for research and teaching in optical sciences and engineering. Here students can obtain a comprehensive education in all areas of optics, leading to an M.S. or Ph.D. in optical sciences or (in collaboration with electrical engineering) a B.S. in optical engineering.

The center's research program and course offerings cover the entire range of optical science, from fundamental optical physics and the development of new optical and electro-optical devices, to lens design and optical system engineering. It has numerous laboratories as well as equipment used for research in a broad range of optics.

Interdisciplinary programs involve the departments of astronomy, biotechnology, chemistry, civil engineering and engineering mechanics, electrical and computer engineering, microbiology, physics, physiology, planetary sciences, and radiology.

Several faculty members have specialties in laser work, including laser system application, laser spectroscopy and laser spectroscopy of solids, holographic techniques, laser physics, pulse propagation in laser amplifiers and attenuators, short-pulse production in lasers, high-energy lasers, and laser amplifiers.

At the OSC, laser analysis has included development of computer models of laser fusion, isotope separation, free-electron lasers, and other complex systems. The free-electron laser model was the first three-dimensional, time-dependent treatment and included detailed interactions between optical and electron beams.

Interested students should write to the Optical Sciences Center, the University of Arizona, Tucson, Arizona, 85721-0094. The website is www.opt-sci.arizona.edu.

University of Central Florida

The University of Central Florida (UCF) Center for Research and Education in Optics and Lasers (CREOL) is an interdisciplinary center formed to provide direct access by Florida's high-tech industry to UCF's program in electro-optics. It is a national leader in the field. Faculty members from the departments of electrical engineering, physics, math, and mechanical engineering work with the program, with a board of directors that includes prominent representatives of local industry. Florida has one of the largest concentrations of electro-optic industrial activity in the United States, with many companies clustered in Orlando.

CREOL was one of the first three independent academic optics departments in the United States. It offers master's and doctoral degrees in optics, photonics, and laser sciences and engineering. In 1999 the program had twenty-five full-time faculty members, as well as twenty-five Ph.D.-level research scientists.

Research is an integral part of CREOL. Several faculty members are studying nonlinear optics, including how extremely high-powered laser radiation interacts with materials. Related projects include using high-intensity light to do optical switching—studies that may have eventual application to optical computing and optical information processing.

Another CREOL program is using various kinds of crystals to change the color of laser light—research that may have medical implications.

CREOL provides students with a wide array of opportunities to pursue research and professional goals. Student chapters of the Optical Society of America (OSA), the IEEE-Lasers and Electro-Optics Society (IEEE-LEOS), and the International Society for Optical Engineering (SPIE) are very active. An impressive feature of CREOL is the eighty-two-thousand-square-foot facility specifically designed for research and education in optics, photonics, and laser sciences and engineering.

For information write to CREOL, College of Optics and Photonics, Box 162700, Orlando, Florida 32816. Or visit its website at www.creol.ucf.edu.

9

JOB HUNTING STRATEGIES AND WORKPLACE AWARENESS

GLOBAL OPPORTUNITIES EXIST for those who seek a career in laser technologies. The prevalence of laser technologies in so many industries calls for growing numbers of trained, dedicated laser professionals. You will need to be trained properly in the science of lasers, as well as in the particulars of the industry that you choose to enter. Whatever route you decide to follow, your search for a career in this field begins with a self-assessment of your own personal qualities.

Personal Characteristics

What type of person will succeed in a career with lasers? To begin with, one who is enthusiastic about math and science. "So much of laser work is related to math and science that you really need to enjoy those fields," said Jack Dyer of the Laser Institute of America. "The more you understand the optical and mathematical principles behind laser operation, the more chance you have to move ahead in the field, rather than merely running the machinery. You can go much further in your career."

It is also important to be able to follow directions precisely. The highly technical nature of working with lasers requires reading and understanding directions exactly and following them to the letter every time. Lasers are unforgiving; if you violate safety standards—even once—you risk permanent damage. Various lasers require different types of protective eyewear. And just because you have gained previous experience with one type of laser does not mean that the same safety standards will automatically work with another type. In one well-publicized case, a research scientist wearing inappropriate eyewear while trying to look into the path of an Nd:YAG laser received a retinal burn after fewer than thirty seconds of exposure.

To succeed in laser technology, especially at the level of technician, you must also be willing to accept responsibility. In a manufacturing plant, for example, you might be one of a handful of laser technicians—or indeed the only technician—among a large number of other workers or machinists. If the equipment breaks down, you've got to get it up and running, no matter what it takes. That may involve trying various ways to repair the machine yourself, contacting manufacturers for assistance, or working with plant engineers. The burden of getting the process back in motion may rest entirely upon you.

No matter what your training has been, you will almost certainly find working with lasers to be an ongoing learning experience. You will need to work on a variety of equipment, and you will gain hands-on experience at the plant or laser site. As new techniques and uses for lasers develop, you will be required to keep up with changes in the field through course work, seminars, after-hours study, and reading trade publications.

Only you can determine whether you truly have the aptitude and personal qualities necessary for a role in this demanding, challenging field. By being honest with yourself about your goals and abilities, you will have a good chance of finding yourself in a career that you truly enjoy. Your self-assessment will also help you to determine where in the field of laser technology you can make your best contribution.

So how do you go about finding your niche? What realistically are your chances of working with lasers? As someone just entering the field in your first job, you may hold one or more jobs within the organization before you work directly with the lasers. The laser represents an enormous investment on the part of the company, so it is unlikely that a beginning technician will be assigned immediately to work with this expensive machine. Instead, a department head is more likely to promote from within, giving someone with more experience the first chance at working with the laser.

Being Selective About Your Training

Although there are many factors that will influence your chances for success, there are some good strategies that you can use to get yourself in a better position. One of them is to be selective about the training you receive. You can find extensive professional course listings on the website for SPIE—the International Society for Optical Engineering (www.spie.org). The programs include short courses and symposia as well as more in-depth programs. You can request the SPIE educational catalog by writing to SPIE, P.O. Box 10, Bellingham, Washington 98227.

When considering colleges, choose carefully. Study their academic programs closely to make sure that they will provide you with the right level of training. Ask about their placement rate for graduates, especially for those who've taken course work in laser technology. Perhaps they will give you the names of one or two alumni in your area whom you can write to or phone. Persons who have studied lasers and who are now working in the field can give you invaluable advice about the preparation you should have and the current job market.

Choose a school or technology program that is accredited by the Accreditation Board for Engineering and Technology (ABET). You can get a list from the board by writing the organization at 111 Market Place, Suite 1050, Baltimore, Maryland 21202. Its website at www.abet.org contains listings of accredited schools and institutes.

Become active in the local student chapters of professional societies (see the list in Appendix A). Keep up with the news on the association's website and get in touch with the appropriate local chapter in your area. Attending meetings will help you learn more about lasers and give you a chance to talk with professionals in the field.

Regularly read three or four of the periodicals listed in the Further Reading section at the end of this book and, if possible, subscribe to them. Not only will you keep up with technological developments, but you will also learn dates of future conferences and seminars. Try to attend these. Often fees for students are extremely low or may be waived with a letter from one of your professors. At these meetings you'll find vendors of various laser products. Pick up catalogs and informative literature as well as business cards of company representatives. Some of them may be willing to talk with you about laser jobs and possible employment. Or they may know of customers who are expanding and who are hiring.

Reading the trade periodicals will give you a list of vendors to contact for literature, so you can keep up with new developments. Each year, many publications run a buyers' guide issue, which includes company names and addresses. You can also check your school or public library for reference publications listing lasers and laser services.

Online Resources

Going online will be one of the most informative as well as enjoyable ways to keep up to date on current developments in laser technology. Nearly every organization, company, or school involved with lasers maintains an Internet website. Many of these sites are quite elaborate, with in-depth explanations of research projects, technical innovations, and commercial applications. For example, the website for Bell Laboratories, at www.bell-labs.com, will provide you with a wealth of information on current investigations in photonics and other laser-related research.

Another outstanding commercial site is that of the magazine *Laser Focus World*, at www.lfw.com. *Laser Focus World* is a leader in the industry and publishes annual reviews and forecasts of the laser industry. The student membership fee is very affordable. You will also be able to access informative career information on this site.

Websites for the professional organizations provide valuable information on educational offerings, conferences, and professional publications. The Society of Manufacturing Engineers (www.sme.org) allows browsers to search by keyword through the thousands of publications indexed on its site. The websites for the Optical Society of America (www.osa.org) and SPIE (www.spie.org) are loaded with helpful information. And you can find information on lasers in medicine by visiting the website for the American Society for

Laser Medicine and Surgery (www.aslms.org). You probably will also want to visit the home page of the Laser Institute (www.laserinstitute.org), where you will find many useful links to laser organizations, manufacturers, and researchers.

Other fascinating sources of information on the World Wide Web include the Web pages of the Department of Defense. Find out about the various military laser programs by searching the DoD's website at www.defenselink.mil.

Résumés

Résumés give you an introduction, show off your strengths, and give you talking points when you're called in for an interview.

When you're job hunting, whether you're a beginner or more experienced, you should highlight significant accomplishments. If you've achieved academic honors, list them. Instead of merely writing down the titles of courses you've taken, indicate the types of laboratory or industrial equipment you've operated, including the types of lasers. Be sure to include your computer literacy—the hardware, software, and languages you've worked with.

If you have worked for only one company, summarize your experience. Be prepared to encapsulate it by listing the two or three most significant things you've done.

Don't get discouraged if you don't get hired immediately by the company of your choice—or even by any company working with lasers. Many companies and managers keep the résumés that placement firms submit. When research and development dollars are approved for a project or a new contract is won, they will know whom they're interested in interviewing.

Salaries and Wages

What can you expect to earn in working with lasers? Research scientists, doctors and dentists, and other professionals working with lasers generally receive very good salaries. Technicians and technologists are employed at both hourly rates and at annual salaries, depending upon the type of job. Unless noted otherwise, the income data for the specialties presented here are from the U.S. Department of Labor's *Occupational Outlook Handbook*, 2006–2007 edition.

- **Skin care specialists.** These are specialists other than medical doctors, such as beauty culturists, manicurists, and pedicurists who perform simple cosmetic procedures such as hair removal. Median annual earnings are $18,500 to $24,010.
- **Manufacturing and industrial.** These machinists use lasers in manufacturing processes. Median hourly earnings are approximately $16.33 per hour. Of these, variations exist by industry: aerospace product and parts manufacturing, $17.78; motor vehicle parts manufacturing, $17.46; metalworking machinery manufacturing, $17.06; and machine shops, turned product, $15.87.

Related manufacturing occupations with similar salaries/wages include: tool and die makers; machine setters, operators, and tenders—metal and plastic; and computer control programmers and operators. Other skilled metalworkers who use laser technology are welders, solderers, and brazers. Almost all of these are union jobs, and a period of apprenticeship at lower wages is required by the unions.

- **Medical technologists and technicians.** Medical technologists and technicians, surgical technicians, and others, as of May

2004, earned a median salary of $38,690. Medical technologists and technicians earned slightly less in private doctors' offices and slightly more in hospital settings.

• **Physicians.** Doctors earned the highest salaries, but with a wide range even in these incomes. Median total compensation of types of physicians who may use laser technology in their practices follows by specialty. These figures are for experienced doctors and are from the Medical Group Management Association, *Physician Compensation and Production Report*, 2005: general surgery, $282,504; obstetrics/gynecology, $247,348; internal medicine, $166,420; pediatrics, $161,331; family practice (without obstetrics), $156,010.

• **Scientists and engineers.** Additional information about engineering salaries is available from the American Association of Engineering Societies (AAES). You can visit its website (www.aaes.org) or write the AAES Engineering Workforce Commission, 1620 I Street, Suite 210, Washington, DC, 20006. These reports can be expensive, so you may want to check with your local college or university library to see if the reports are available there.

Another source of information on salaries for scientists and engineers is the National Science Foundation (NSF). All NSF reports are available free of charge on the World Wide Web. For information, go to www.nsf.gov. The salary reports published by the Science Resources Studies Division are published annually and contain much valuable information about employment trends.

There are very substantial differences in salaries among workers in the same field, depending on level of education and years of experience. In 2006, the NIF reported median annual salaries of scientists and engineers employed full-time (from the data available for the year 2003) for younger scientists and engineers (age twenty-nine years or younger) were $39,000 (bachelor's degree holders) and

$45,000 (master's degree holders). For scientists and engineers age fifty and older, median salaries were reported as $57,000 (bachelor's degree holders) and $86,500 (master's degree holders).

This report also gives data for individual occupations within the categories, and it shows separate median amounts tabulated for females and males in the different groups. It is important to note that, in general, the median salaries for females in all age groups and all categories are lower than those for males. The complete report can be accessed at www.nif.gov, Table H-16.

If your work steadily improves, you can expect your wages to rise steadily the longer you are employed because, as long as the economy is in good shape, companies and other employers try to give productive employees at least a cost-of-living raise each year, and most do more than that. Merit increases following outstanding contributions to the organization may be in the form of bonuses or salary increases.

Don't forget the business side of lasers as you consider opportunities in laser technology. Companies offering laser products and services need communications and marketing, as well as product sales and support staff—knowledgeable men and women who can talk to customers about their needs and can make recommendations that may ultimately result in sales. Backgrounds useful for obtaining those positions will include marketing and sales training, as well as enough science and technology to understand customer problems and the products being offered.

Licenses and Certifications

In all fifty U.S. states and in Canada, many of the occupations involving lasers are required by law to be licensed or certified. These include jobs as operators, technicians, technologists, nurse assistants, dental assistants, surgeons, therapists, doctors and dentists, and others in the fields of beauty culture and cosmetology, skin care, plastic surgery, general surgery, oncology, podiatry, dentistry, and others who use lasers and laser-related equipment.

In the United States and Canada the state or province's department of licensure and regulation (or a similar title) will provide information about rules and regulations, testing, and certification or licensing that is required. Fees are usually charged for the testing, licenses, and periodic renewals, often on a yearly basis. Continuing education may also be required to maintain the license in a current state, once it is issued.

Manufacturers often supply certification courses, but these certifications are not the same as those required by the various governments. You will need to contact your government offices and request the forms and regulations that apply in your area.

Safety Regulations and OSHA

A variety of important safety regulations apply to laser use in different circumstances in laboratories, factories, hospitals and clinics, and other environments. They may have a variety of origins, such as professional organizations, individual manufacturers of equipment, individual employers, or simply from the members of a particular team. They may also be regulations of local, county, state, and national governments. You will be expected to be familiar with the regulations that apply to your profession, and you may be asked about them during job interviews.

In the United States, the U.S. Department of Labor's Occupational Safety and Health Administration (OSHA) maintains government safety standards that must be met, and it is the individual's responsibility to learn what OSHA standards apply to specific equipment use and activity. Owners and managers of companies have OSHA responsibilities, and the details are carefully defined in OSHA publications.

In most instances, the relevant OSHA regulations must be posted or otherwise made available at the job site. For more information, contact OSHA at www.osha.gov.

An OSHA technical manual specifically includes material for laser safety and is published as *OSHA Technical Manual* Section III: "Chapter 6: Laser Hazards." Its sections include:

1. Introduction
2. Nonbeam Laser Hazards
3. Biological Effects of the Laser Beam
4. Laser Hazard Classifications
5. Investigational Guidelines
6. Control Measures, Safety Programs
7. Bibliography

Nearly all countries have similar governmental and professional organizations that provide safety and security oversight, standards, and rules and regulations. Whether you are a student, a job applicant, or a new employee, you will need to research these organizations and their requirements if you plan to work with lasers in another country.

10

WOMEN AND MINORITIES IN SCIENCE AND TECHNOLOGY

LASER TECHNOLOGY IS in itself a relatively new field, and it is inextricably linked to the fields of science and technology in general. Traditionally, women and minority groups have not been able to participate as equals in these fields, and the Civil Rights Act of 1964, the Equal Opportunity Act, the Americans with Disabilities Act in 1990, and other legislation in more recent years were passed in an attempt to help remedy that inequity. A variety of organizations and associations have also made attempts to help women and minority group members take part fully, both as students and as professionals.

In 2006, there were 118 million women in the United States, and 70 percent of those were considered to be in the workforce, either employed or actively looking for work.

According to the United States Department of Labor's 2004 statistics, women made up 46 percent of the total workforce, and this amount was projected to rise only a small amount to 47 percent by the year 2014.

Also in 2004, the Commission on Professionals in Science and Technology released a report on women in science and technology that found that gains "for women in science, technology, engineering, and mathematics (STEM) occupations have been uneven." It stated that the number of women's jobs in the STEM areas had not increased, and the proportion of jobs held by women in computer science and mathematics had decreased between 1983 and 2003.

Salaries and wages had shown even less progress, and the gap between women's and men's wages had actually gotten larger, with pay for women being 81 percent of that of men's in 1995, and only 78.7 percent in 2003.

A similar report was issued by the commission in 2005 on participation of minorities in STEM occupations from 1994 to 2004. The results of this study showed small but steady gains for Latino populations but a plateau for African Americans. Although Latinos had made steady gains, they still accounted for only 3.7 percent of the STEM jobs in 1994 and 5.3 percent in 2004. For African Americans the proportion seemed to have peaked at 6.2 percent in 1999 to 2001 and stayed approximately the same since then. Compared to their shares of the total population, 12.9 percent for Latinos and 10.7 percent for African Americans, they are seriously underrepresented in the total numbers of STEM jobs.

Enrollment Demographics

In recent years, the effects of civil rights legislation, upward mobility of families, increasing expectations, and other factors can be seen in changes in minority education and job patterns.

In 1978, the percentage of all adults who had had at least some postsecondary education was 37 percent; by 2002 that percentage had reached 61 percent. Not all of these had completed a certificate or degree, but the change indicated better preparation for the workforce and for life in general.

According to the National Center for Educational Statistics in the report *Postsecondary Participation Rates by Sex and Race/Ethnicity: 1974–2003*, participation by women in all ethnic groups increased during the period from 1974 to 2003 and outdistanced the men. The groups studied were black men and women, Latino men and women, and white men and women. Of the six groups, only Latino men lost ground, and a smaller percentage of them were participating in postsecondary education by 2003. The entire report can be accessed at www.nces.gov.

Students with disabilities—learning disabilities, orthopedic disabilities, and others—represented less than 3 percent of all college freshmen in 1978 but more than 9 percent in 2000. Students reporting learning disabilities accounted for the increase, while the numbers of students reporting visual impairments and orthopedic impairments actually decreased. Data are incomplete for this group of students because most schools do not keep records indicating disabilities of individual student populations unless the students themselves report it, and many do not keep records of disabilities at all.

Current data and historical trends related to the education of women and minorities in the sciences are compiled by the National Science Foundation (NSF). A detailed report by the NSF Division of Science Resources Studies entitled *Women, Minorities, and Persons with Disabilities in Science and Engineering* is available online at www.nsf.org.

Concentrate on Science and Math

If you are a woman or a member of a minority group, what can you do to become qualified to work with lasers? One important strategy is to excel in science and mathematics. As a junior high or high school student, sign up for all the math and science possible. Often, especially in large metropolitan areas such as Chicago or Atlanta, there are opportunities for enrichment programs in those subjects. Even if such programs require your after-school, weekend, or vacation time, take advantage of everything you can. The skills you gain and the contacts you make can be invaluable. Also, as you begin to read about schools with engineering or optics programs, write to the director of admissions at those institutions that interest you. Ask about summer studies, minority recruitment, or special programs you can join.

Math and science are two important tools you'll need to qualify for jobs working with lasers. Optics and electro-optics are demanding sciences. Finding opportunities for additional study and taking advantage of them may give you the edge you need for admission to a top-quality college or university program.

Additional Resources

Society of Women Engineers

The Society of Women Engineers (SWE) is an organization dedicated to helping women who choose to pursue careers in engineering. The society also tracks the achievements and statistics of women in this field and sponsors numerous educational programs (including a unique e-mail mentoring program) and more than ninety scholarships. These scholarships range in amount and are open only to women who are majoring in engineering or computer science. To receive information about the scholarships, send a self-addressed envelope to Society of Women Engineers Headquarters, 230 East Ohio Street, Chicago, Ilinois 60611, or go to www.swe.org. You also can write to the SWE for information on joining one of the local student chapters, which are located throughout the United States.

The website for the SWE, which can be found online at www .swe.org, is an excellent resource for women of all ages who are considering pursuing a career in engineering. Among the resources you will find are "Career Guidance Tools," which will help you choose the best science curriculum for your plan of study.

American Council on Education

The American Council on Education (ACE) is another educational organization that collects and publishes information on education. In 1987, ACE launched its Minority Initiative in response to declining rates of minority participation in higher education. The Office of Minorities in Higher Education (OMHE), which is part of ACE, is a major source of information on the education status of minorities. Through OMHE you can also learn about those programs that serve underrepresented minority students. Every other year the OMHE sponsors an important national conference on diversity and improving minority participation in postsecondary education called "Educating All of One Nation."

To find out more about the OMHE, write to the Office of Minorities in Higher Education, American Council on Education, One Dupont Circle NW, Washington, DC 20036. You can visit the ACE website at www.acenet.edu, where you will find information on minority programs as well as programs for women.

Other associations that especially support women and minorities include the Association for Women in Science and Technology (www.awis.org) and the Society for Canadian Women in Science and Technology (www.scwist.ca).

The National Science Foundation (www.nsf.gov) provides extensive studies and reports, general information about schools and training programs, grants and scholarships, and comprehensive data on science activities in the United States.

An excellent online resource is Cyberg (www.edu-cyberg.com/teachers/womenminoritiestech.html). Go to its website for a variety of free resources for science and technological jobs and careers for women and minorities.

11

INTERNATIONAL OPPORTUNITIES

LASER TECHNOLOGY IS a growing part of the intellectual and economic activity in nearly every country of the world, and research
and new applications are noticeably taking place in Austria, Bel-
gium, China, Denmark, Egypt, France, Germany, Greece, India,
Iran, Israel, Italy, Japan, Jordan, the Netherlands, Norway, Portu-
gal, Russia, Singapore, South Korea, Spain, Sweden, Switzerland,
Syria, and many other countries.

Some detail is provided in this chapter about the activity in the
English-speaking countries of Canada, Britain, and Australia. In
addition, you will find names of professional associations and of
universities and research centers in many other countries in Appen-
dixes A and B.

The global nature of the laser technology revolution adds to its
importance and its great interest at this time in history. You will

want to gain an overview of the activity worldwide and perhaps also investigate further one or more of the countries that especially interest you.

Laser Technology in Canada

Lasers and related technology play an important part in Canadian research and development. Research activity is growing at many locations, and a new national project, the ALLS Project, was announced in 2004.

The ALLS Project

The Advanced Laser Light Source, or ALLS, Project is to develop a multibeam femtosecond laser system comprised of five lasers, which can function at a wide range of wavelengths. This first-ever, state-of-the-art multibeam laser system makes Canada a world leader in this kind of research, and it will be used in a variety of important areas, including biology, chemistry, medicine, and physics for such important work as breast cancer detection.

The Canadian government has awarded a fund of $20 million for the research project to involve eight leading Canadian universities and to be administered by Dr. Jean-Claude Kieffer at the University of Quebec's Institute of Scientific Research. Scientists from key institutions in Austria, France, Germany, Greece, Italy, Japan, Sweden, and the United States are also involved.

At the University of Toronto, a team of renowned professors are involved with research in lasers and related topics. The department is host to a number of international meetings each year, and the science and optics program is of very high quality.

Alberta Laser Centre

At the University of Alberta, research in laser technology has been pursued since the mid-1960s. The Alberta Laser Institute, established in 1984, has fostered research in various laser applications, concentrating on industrial applications, and current programs also involve robotics, materials processing, laser sensors, electronics, and medical applications. Facilities include state-of-the-art CAD/CAM-based laser manufacturing capabilities that include cutting, heat treating, cladding, welding, and drilling—processes that are used on materials as diverse as ceramic, plastic, rubber, glass, wood, textile, paper, and electronic circuit fabrication elements.

Laser research is being conducted under the aegis of the program of condensed matter physics. An annual event is the Lake Louise Winter Institute in Physics in the majestic natural setting of the Canadian Rockies at Banff.

For more information on the National Laser Research and Development Projects in Canada, contact:

Office of the Ministry of Industry
Minister of the Crown
Canadian Cabinet
C.D. Howe Building
235 Queen Street
Ottawa, Ontario
Canada K1A OH5

Laser Technology in Great Britain

Opportunities for careers in laser technology in Britain have been expanding as rapidly as those in the United States. Lasers are used in manufacturing, surgery, communications, defense applications, and metrology (the science of measurement).

Oxford University

Oxford University is a world leader in research in the areas of x-ray lasers, radiative transfer, pico-second x-ray diffraction, dense plasmas, and parametric instabilities, among others. Justin Wark's Research Group and Oxford High Power Laser Group at Clarendon Laboratory are well known. For more information, go online to www.laserplasma.physics.ox.ac.uk.

Industrial Production

British industry has embraced laser technology for many applications. One British firm, Laser Scientific Services Ltd., in Cambridgeshire, England, developed the technology of laser-cutting large aluminum aircraft panels in three dimensions. Technicians at the factory operate computer-programmed lasers to cut central slots and panel profiles for strategic aircraft. Complex geometric shapes are cut in panels of various materials, using a sophisticated digitizer and computer-aided program system that has direct numerical control.

Laser Scientific Services Ltd., which sells, installs, and maintains industrial laser systems, also uses a computer numerically controlled (CNC) laser to make cuts with precise repeatability. A wide range of plastic, metal, laminate, and composite materials can be used. Other activities include cutting, profiling, scribing, or drilling of ceramic components for the microelectronics industry.

For additional information about laser use in the United Kingdom, contact:

Electronic Engineering Association
Leicester House
8 Leicester Street
London WC2H 7BN
United Kingdom

British Medical Association
Tavistock Square
London WCI 9JP
United Kingdom

Laser Technology in Australia

Australia has a strong tradition of research and development in mining, biomedical sciences, and scientific instrumentation, which is reflected in a high level of laser research and development, applications, and manufacturing.

Macquarie University

A key center for laser research and development has been established at Macquarie University in New South Wales, under the direction of Professor Jim Piper, a world-renowned laser physicist. Researchers investigate the basic science of laser physics while tailoring technology for specific applications and manufacturing within Australia. The center also emphasizes medical applications of lasers for therapeutic diagnostics and for surgery.

Materials Processing and Medical Lasers

Australia has invested much in laser development efforts for materials processing and medical lasers. Most of the industrial lasers are integrated with computer numerically controlled systems. Medical lasers include CO_2 lasers to metal vapor lasers developed in Australia. Copper and gold and other metal vapor lasers have also been marketed. Joint projects have been carried out with Monash University and the University of Colorado in the United States, among others.

Physicians at major hospitals and medical centers are using various types of lasers for dermatology, cancer surgery, gynecology, and photodynamic laser therapy.

Training Opportunities

Government officials continue to review the state of lasers in Australia. In the late 1980s it was determined that there was an identifiable need for laser technologists who could gain their skills by one- to two-year associations with existing laser research and development facilities. At the University of New South Wales, training in lasers and optics is offered in the third year of physics training.

Other universities offer postgraduate courses related to lasers. A center for laser physics operates at the Australian National University, Canberra, with a focus on mechanisms of laser fusion. Conventional Nd:YAG performance has been considerably improved during the course of this work, and this has found its way into the products of the company, Electro-Optic Systems, which won a large contract from the U.S. Department of Defense for a series of laser radar systems. Research by postgraduate students is also being done at a number of other universities.

The CUDOS Program

A major national research program is being carried out in CUDOS—the Centre for Ultrahigh Bandwidth Devices for Optical Systems—with teams working with Scottish universities, St. Andrews, Oxford, and South Hampton.

For more information on lasers and laser training in Australia, contact:

Centre for Lasers and Applications
Macquarie University
North Ryde, New South Wales 2113
Australia
www.ics.mq.edu.au/cla

Centre for Laser Research and Applications
University of New South Wales
Sydney, New South Wales 2052
Australia
www.unsw.edu.au

Appendix A

Professional Societies and Associations

Because laser technology spans a great breadth of applications, many trade associations are involved with its varied aspects. Provided here are descriptions of several of the largest and most important of the trade associations in the United States and Canada, plus an extended list, with websites, of many more in countries throughout the world.

The websites provide a wealth of information, and membership provides even more. Some of the associations provide reduced membership rates for students. Most sponsor important conferences and meetings that students can attend for reduced fees. Nearly all have journals, magazines, and other publications, and often these are available to students at discounted rates. Many associations offer career guidance information as well as job announcements and networking services. In addition, many offer videotapes, CDs, and DVDs about their special areas of the industry that can be borrowed or rented.

There are many advantages to joining a professional association while you are still in school. Meetings and networking can be very beneficial. Serving on a committee, even while a student, provides recognition and learning experiences.

American Society for Laser Medicine and Surgery

This professional association of several thousand members in the United States and other countries is dedicated to the exchange of information concerning medical lasers. Members include physicists who develop devices, biomedical engineers who adapt them for practical purposes, safety officers who supervise the working of lasers, biologists who study the effects of laser energy on living tissue, and health professionals who treat patients with lasers.

The American Society for Laser Medicine and Surgery (ASLMS) has formulated standards and guidelines for safe, effective laser programs in hospitals and other institutions and for those who conduct both basic and advanced courses. The ASLMS informs its members about postgraduate courses and training programs in laser biology, nursing, medicine, and surgery.

In association with other national, regional, international, and specialty laser societies, the ASLMS cooperates with the International Congress of Lasers in Surgery and Medicine, the Laser Institute of America, and the Society of Photo-Optical Instrumentation Engineers (SPIE) in organizing programs.

For more information on ASLMS, go to www.aslms.org.

Institute of Industrial Engineers

The Institute of Industrial Engineers (IIE) is a major international professional society. Its thousands of members are concerned with the design, improvement, and installation of integrated systems of people, material, information, equipment, and energy—all the elements in the "productivity" equation.

Two major conferences yearly (the Annual International Industrial Engineering Conference and Show and the Fall Industrial Engineering Conference), plus numerous seminars, continuing education programs, and workshops are sponsored.

Through its career guidance program, IIE acquaints thousands of young people each year with the opportunities of a career in industrial engineering and awards scholarships and fellowships to outstanding student members at both graduate and undergraduate levels.

For more information on IIE, go to www.iienet.org.

International Association of Machinists and Aerospace Workers

The union and trade association of the machinists and aerospace workers was famously built to a significant force in labor by its late leader, William ("Wimpy") Winpisinger. The International Association of Machinists and Aerospace Workers (IAMAW) today embraces a membership of more than 730,000 in all fifty states plus ten provinces and three territories in Canada.

The union has headquarters in Maryland and maintains the large William Winpisinger Memorial Education Center in Georgia. It carries on collective bargaining and provides member courses in personal finance, new manufacturing and communications technology and media, labor and human rights, safety and health, and leadership. It has an active nonpartisan political organization, and its members maintain a strong political presence in labor and human rights agendas.

For more information on IAMAW, go to www.goiam.org.

Laser Institute of America

The Laser Institute of America (LIA) is a nonprofit professional society for the advancement and promotion of laser technology and applications. It conducts continuing education courses, seminars, and technical symposia and offers a variety of educational materials and publications, including the *Journal of Laser Applications*, *Laser Safety Guide*, and *LIA Today*. Student chapters are found at many colleges, universities, and technical institutes.

LIA cosponsors an important major annual conference on lasers: ICALEO, the International Congress on Applications of Lasers and Electro-Optics, in cooperation with the American Society for Laser Medicine and Surgery; the Society of Manufacturing Engineers; the International Society of Podiatric Laser Surgery; the American Society of Metals, International; the Midwest Bio-Laser Institute; the High Temperature Society of Japan; the Western Institute for Laser Treatment; the Japan Laser Processing Society; the Japan Society for Laser Technology; and IFS Conferences Ltd.

ICALEO features four simultaneous technical conferences: Laser Materials Processing, Laser Research in Medicine, Optical Methods in Flow and Particle Diagnostics, and Electro-Optic Sensing and Measurement.

LIA works closely with other laser-related organizations to coordinate courses for professionals that are offered at various locations throughout the country.

For more information on LIA, go to www.laserinstitute.org.

Optical Society of America

The Optical Society of America (OSA) has more than fourteen thousand individual members, including scientists, engineers, and technicians from the United States and fifty other countries. Members work in industry, educational institutions, and government agencies and include a number of Nobel laureates. Students may join at a reduced rate.

Among the Optical Society of America's publications is its news magazine, *Optics and Photonics News.* In addition, OSA publishes foreign journals translated into English, such as *Chinese Physics—Lasers, Optics, and Spectroscopy*, and the *Soviet Journal of Optical Technology.*

For more information on OSA, go to www. osa.org.

Society of Manufacturing Engineers

The Society of Manufacturing Engineers (SME) is one of the largest professional engineering associations in the world, with more than seventy thousand members and hundreds of chapters worldwide. It has more than ten thousand student members and more than 240 student chapters.

Within SME, various associations are concerned with different aspects of the manufacturing industry. As the umbrella organization, SME annually sponsors more than 150 special programs, 50 technical conferences, 40 expositions, and 500 symposia and workshops. It publishes technical papers and maintains an online electronic database search service, which is available through the society's library.

SME has a laser council composed of industry leaders experienced in use of lasers in manufacturing, which plans an intensive annual conference that features research papers and reports on laser technology and applications.

For more information on SME, go to www.sme.org.

International Society of Optical Engineering (SPIE)

Formerly called the Society of Photo-Optical Instrumentation Engineers, SPIE changed its name but kept its original acronym and mission. SPIE is dedicated to advancing engineering and scientific applications of optical, electro-optical, and opto-electronic instrumentation, systems, and technology. Its 17,500 members include scientists, engineers, and users. SPIE provides publications and conferences to communicate new developments and applications to the scientific, engineering, and user communities.

For more information on SPIE, go to www.spie.org.

Additional Laser-Related Associations Around the World

Many American associations have become international in recent years, and many associations of other countries have become regional and global as well. The following list offers a sample of associations in many countries and provides a starting point for an appreciation of the size and depth of this industry worldwide.

- American Welding Society, www.aws.org
- Association of Industrial Laser Users, www.ailu.org.uk
- Association of Laser Safety Professionals, www.laserprotectionadviser.com
- Association of Laser Users, The, www.ailu.org.uk
- British Medical Laser Association, www.bmla.co.uk
- China Optics and Optoelectronics Manufactures Association, www.coema.org.cn/english.htm
- Dermatological Society of Singapore, www.dermatology.org

- Electronic Industries Association of Korea, www.eiak.org
- Engineering Technology Teachers Association, www.etta.ie
- EUnited Robotics—European Robotics Association, www.eu-nited-robotics.net
- European Laser Association, www.europeanlaser.org
- European Laser Institute, www.europeanlaserinstitute.org
- European Renewable Energy Centres Agency, www.eurec.be
- European Union-Developing Countries Laser Processing Initiative, www.eudevlas.eu
- Federal Ministry of Education and Research—Germany, www.bmbf.de, English language site
- FTA Flexographic Technical Association, www.flexography.org
- Hong Kong Surgical Laser Association, The, www.hkslaser.com
- Indian Laser Association, The, www.ila.org.in
- International Association of Machinists and Aerospace Workers, www.goiam.org
- International Hologram Manufactures Association—IHMA, www.ihma.org
- International Laser Display Association, www.laserist.org
- International Laser Tag Association, www.lasertag.org
- International Laser Technology Congress AKL 2008, http://www.lasercongress.org
- Japan Laser Processing Society, www.jlps.gr.jp, Japanese language site
- Laser Florence—the Laser Medicine World, www.laserflorence.org
- LaserFocusWorld, www.laserfocusworld.org

- Laser Training Institute, www.lasertraining.org
- Max-Planck Society, The, www.mpg.de/english, Comprises more than sixty institutes and other facilities (German-language site)
- Metal Etching Technology, www.metassocs.com/history
- Multifunction Products Association, www.mfpa.org
- North American Association for Laser Therapy, www.naalt.org
- Optical Storage Technology Association, www.osta.org
- Optoelectronics Industry Development Association, www.oida.org
- World Association for Laser Therapy, www.walt.nu

International List of Schools and Research Institutes

Worldwide, hundreds of institutions offer study that prepares students for careers in laser technology. Community colleges, online schools, colleges, universities, technical institutes, professional associations, research centers, and equipment manufacturers provide many choices—from seminars and certificate courses to two-year associate and four-year degrees, masters, doctorates, postdoctoral study, and other advanced work.

Following is a selected list of four-year and graduate schools and research institutes, included for their quality of general science education, physics, and/or laser technology programs; the quality of their faculty and research; and/or participation in laser-technology intern programs, conferences, advanced research, and related events. If a school that interests you is not on this list, it is not an indication that the school is of lesser quality. This is by no means an exhaustive list but is provided for a broad overview of the many choices available. The schools listed are on six continents and offer study in different languages. Each has a website accessible by searching with its name.

Academia Sinica–Taiwan
African Laser Centre–Johannesburg
American University
Appalachian State University
Argonne National Laboratory
Arizona State University
Arizona Western College
Auburn University
Australian National University
Barnard College
Bartol Research Institute
Baylor University
Bhabha Atomic Research Centre
Binghamton University–SUNY
Bogazici University
Boise State University
Boston College
Boston University
Bowdoin College
Brandeis University
Brigham Young University
Brown University
Bryn Mawr College
Bucknell University
California Institute of Technology
California State University–Fresno
Canadian Institute for Theoretical Astrophysics

Cardiff University
Carnegie Institution of Washington
Carnegie Mellon University
Case Western Reserve University
Catholic University of America
Centre for Space Physics–Kolkata, India
CERN—European Organization for Nuclear Research
Chalmers University of Technology
Charles University–Prague
Chiba University
Chinese Academy of Sciences
Chinese University of Hong Kong
Chungnam National University
Chuo University
City University of New York
Clemson University
Colby College
Colgate University
College of Wooster
Colorado State University
Columbia University
Connecticut College
Connecticut State University
Copenhagen University Observatory
Copernicus Astronomical Centre
Cornell University
Danish Space Research Institute, The
Dartmouth College
Davidson College
Dickinson College

Dominion Astrophysical Observatory
Drew University
Drexel University
Duke University
Durham University
East Tennessee State University
Eastern Michigan University
Emory University
European Space Agency Centre
Fayetteville State University
Fermi National Accelerator Laboratory
Florida Institute of Technology
Florida State University
Francis Marion University
Franklin and Marshall College
George Mason University
George Washington University
Georgetown University
Georgia Institute of Technology
Georgia Southern University
Georgia State University
Gunma Astronomical Observatory
Hampden-Sydney College
Harvard University
Harvard-Smithsonian Center for Astrophysics
Harvey Mudd College
Hebrew University of Jerusalem
Heidelberg College, USA
Herzberg Institute of Astrophysics
Hiroshima University

Hong Kong University of Science and Technology
Hope College
Hosei University
Howard University
University of Pennsylvania
Illinois Institute of Technology
Illinois Wesleyan University
Imperial College–London
Indian Institute of Astrophysics
Indiana University
Innsbruck University
Institut D'astrophysique de Paris
Institute of Theoretical Science–Mexico
Instituto de Fisica de Cantabria
International School for Advanced Studies
Iowa State University
Istanbul University
Johns Hopkins University
Kanazawa University
Kansas State University
Kapteyn Astronomical Institute
Keele University
Kent State University
Kenyon College
King's College London
Korea Astronomy Observatory
Kyoto University
Laboratoire D'astrophysique–Marseille
Lafayette College
Lancaster University

Lawrence Berkeley National Laboratory
Lawrence Livermore National Laboratory
Leyden University
Los Alamos National Laboratory
Louisiana State University
Lowell Observatory
Luther College
Macalester College
Marquette University
Massachusetts Institute of Technology
Max-Planck-Institut Für Astrophysik
Max-Planck-Institut Für Physik
McGill University
McMaster University
Miami University of Ohio
Michigan State University
Middle East Technical University
Middle Tennessee State University
Mississippi State University
Miyazaki University
Montana State University
Mullard Space Science Laboratory
Nagoya University
Nanyang Technological University
National Astronomical Observatory–Japan
National Institute of Technology–Hamirpur
National Observatory of Athens
National Tsing Hua University
National University of Singapore
Netherlands Institute for Space Research

New Jersey Institute of Technology
New Mexico Institute of Mining/Technology
New Mexico State University
New York University
Niels Bohr Institute
Nihon Fukushi University
Nihon University
North Carolina State University
Northeastern University
Northwestern University
Oberlin University
Observatoire Royal de Belgique
Ohio State University, The
Ohio University
Oregon State University
Osaka University
Osservatorio Astronomico di Palermo
Oxford University
Palo Alto Research Laboratory
Paul Scherrer Institute
Pedagogical University, Institute of Physics–Kielce, Poland
Pennsylvania State University, The
Pomona College
Portland State University
Princeton University
Prism Computational Sciences
Purdue University
Queen's University
Raman Research Institute
Reed College

Rensselaer Polytechnic Institute
Rhodes College
Rice University
Rochester Institute of Technology
Royal Observatory–Edinburgh
Rutgers University
Rutherford Appleton Laboratory
Sabanci University
Saitama University
San Diego State University
Seoul National University
Shanghai Astronomical Observatory
Shibaura Institute of Technology
Siena College
Simon Fraser University
Skidmore College
Smithsonian Astrophysical Observatory
S. N. Bose National Centre for Basic Sciences–Kolkata,
    India
Sonoma State University
South African Astronomical Observatory
Southern Ilinois University at Carbondale
Southern Methodist University
Spitzer Science Center
Stanford University
State University of New York–Albany
Sternberg Astronomical Institute
Stockholms Universitet
Stony Brook University
Sussex University

Swarthmore College
Swedish Institute of Space Physics
Swinburne University of Technology
Swiss Federal Institute of Technology–Zurich
Syracuse University
Tata Institute of Fundamental Research
Technical University of Munich
Technion-Israel Institute of Technology
Tel Aviv University
Temple University
Tennessee State University
Tesre/Cnr Toho University
Texas A&M University
Texas Christian University
Texas Technical University
Tohoku University
Tokai University
Tokyo University of Science
Trinity College Dublin
Tsukuba Space Center
Tufts University
Tuskegee University
Union College
Universidad Complutense de Madrid
Universidad de Chile
Universidade do Sao Paulo
Universidade Federal do Rio Grande do Sul
Universitat Hamburg
Universiteit Ghent
Universiteit Van Amsterdam

University at Buffalo
University College–Dublin
University College–London
University of Alabama
University of Alberta
University of Amsterdam
University of Arizona
University of Arkansas–Little Rock
University of Athens
University of Birmingham
University of Bochum
University of Bristol
University of British Columbia
University of Calgary
University of California–Santa Barbara
University of California–Berkeley
University of California–Los Angeles
University of California–San Francisco
University of Central Lancashire
University of Chicago
University of Colorado
University of Connecticut
University of Copenhagen
University of Crete
University of Delaware
University of Denver
University of Edinburgh
University of Florida
University of Georgia
University of Hawaii

University of Hawaii–Hilo
University of Hawaii–Manoa
University of Hawaii–West O'ahu
University of Heidelberg
University of Helsinki
University of Hertfordshire
University of Houston
University of Urbana/Champaign
University of Illinois–Chicago
University of Iowa
University of Kansas
University of Kentucky
University of Leeds
University of Leicester
University of Liege
University of Lodz
University of Louisville
University of Manchester
University of Manitoba
University of Maryland
University of Massachusetts
University of Melbourne
University of Miami
University of Michigan
University of Minnesota
University of Mississippi
University of Missouri–Columbia
University of Montana
University of Montreal
University of Nebraska

University of Nevada
University of New Hampshire
University of New South Wales
University of Newcastle
University of North Carolina
University of North Dakota
University of North Texas
University of Notre Dame
University of Nottingham
University of Oklahoma
University of Oregon
University of Oxford
University of Pennsylvania
University of Queensland
University of Richmond
University of Rochester
University of San Francisco
University of Science/Technology of China
University of Sheffield
University of South Carolina
University of Southampton
University of Southern California
University of St. Andrews
University of Sydney
University of Tasmania
University of Tennessee
University of Texas–Austin
University of Toledo
University of Toronto
University of Turku

University of Utah
University of Vermont
University of Victoria
University of Vienna
University of Virginia
University of Washington
University of Washington–Seattle
University of Wisconsin
University of Wyoming
Utrecht University
Vanderbilt University
Villanova University
Virginia Polytechnic
Washington University–St. Louis
Wayne State University
Wesleyan University
West Virginia University
Western Kentucky University
Whittier College
Yale University
Yamagata University
Yunnan Astronomical Observatory

FURTHER READING

LASER TECHNOLOGY IS developing so rapidly that you will want to keep up with news and events. To stay on top of current developments, you will want to read the professional and scientific publications that cover new discoveries and applications, and you also will find that using the Internet as a reference tool will provide you with access to many materials that you would not otherwise be able to obtain.

Library Resources

Libraries have been and remain an invaluable resource for information gathering and research. The topic of lasers is a specialized and technical one, and the following services offered by libraries may prove helpful to you.

Interlibrary Loans

Libraries in large metropolitan areas frequently provide services under which they share information. A number of public libraries belong to an interlibrary consortium that makes photocopies of articles you can't find at your local library and sends them to your local librarian at no charge to you.

Special Databases and Other Library Reference Aids

Reference librarians often are tied in with various databases. Because you are a cardholder at your local library, the library may be willing to do a certain number of free or low-cost searches per year on topics related to lasers. If you are requesting a special reference search that will take a significant amount of time, check first with your librarian to see whether there is a charge for the service.

Internet

Still another way in which you may get material on lasers is through computer searching. This is usually the handiest and fastest way to get an introduction to the field. Some outstanding websites are given in this book, and you may also want to keep notes of others you find that are of special interest to you.

Periodicals

Thousands of periodicals, including newspapers, magazines, academic and professional journals, and newsletters are published in the United States and in most other countries on a regular basis.

They form an enormous pool of information and opinion that is highly valuable.

Specialized and General Interest Publications

Some of the periodicals listed here will probably be too specialized to be found in most public libraries; however, they may be included in the holdings of local colleges or universities, or they can be obtained through interlibrary loan. Speak with your reference librarian to find out how to request materials from affiliated libraries if your library does not subscribe to the particular journal or magazine that you want to read. Another way to get up-to-date information is to use library indexes. You have probably already used the *Reader's Guide to Periodical Literature*, an index commonly found in public libraries that tracks articles in many popular magazines by subject matter.

In addition, most libraries have companion indexes, which are organized along similar lines. The *Business Periodicals Index* focuses on magazines and publications of interest in commercial, financial, and economic fields. You can look up "lasers" in recent volumes of *BPI*, and then go to the individual publications that are listed there for particular articles. Stories and news you would find about lasers might include material on company profits, mergers and acquisitions, lawsuits, or future sales.

By gaining an understanding of activity in the industry, you will get an awareness of the general health of the job market and where new job opportunities might be concentrated. Corporations that are growing will be hiring more than those without new activity taking place and vice versa: corporations that are in a downturn will not be hiring very much, if at all.

A good way to keep up with technical advances in laser technology is to use the *Applied Science and Technology Index*. Here the broad topic of lasers is subdivided into such headings as "Lasers—Industrial Applications," "Laser Printers," and "Lasers—Measurement Methods."

Each of these indexes provides a list of the periodicals covered, with an address and subscription rate for each. You will find that certain publications show up frequently in these indexes. If your library does not subscribe to a magazine you need, you may want to order it from the publisher directly.

Companies that manufacture, sell, or service equipment in electronics, physics, or telecommunications may possibly have corporate libraries. Your public library reference librarian may also know of other special libraries that are available in your area and whom to call to find out what print and multimedia materials they may have. Often if a magazine is expensive or is so specialized that a public library doesn't subscribe to it, individual corporations will have copies you can look at.

Selected List of Journals and Other Periodicals

Here is a list of some of the most famous and established of the journals and other periodicals that are related to this field. The Web address is provided for each one. By looking at the home pages, you will get a good idea of what's included in the periodical; in many cases, complete issues or selected articles are available online.

American Journal of Physics, www.scitation.aip.org
Applied Optics, www.ieee.org
Fiber and Integrated Optics, www.tandf.co.uk/journals

IEEE Journal of Quantum Electronics, www.ieee.org

IEEE Photonics Technology, www.ieee.org

Industrial Laser Solutions, www.industrial-lasers.com

International Society for Optical Engineering Publications,
    www.spie.org

Journal of Applied Physics, www.jap.aip.org

Journal of Biomedical Optics, www.spie.org

Journal of Laser Applications, www.scitation.aip.org/jla

Journal of Nonlinear Optical Physics and Materials,
    www.sciencedirect.com/science/journal

Journal of Russian Laser Research,
    www.periodicals.com/Springer

Laser Chemistry, www.hindawi.com/journal

Laser Focus World, www.laserfocusworld.com

Laser and Particle Beams, www.journal.cambridge.org

Laser Physics, www.lasphys.com

Lasers in Engineering, www.oldcitypublishing.com/lie

Lasers and Optronics, www.mondotimes.com

Medical Technology Insight, www.medtechinsight.com

Optical Engineering, www.spie.org

Optical and Quantum Electronics,
    www.springer.com/west/home/physics

Optics Communications, www.elsevier.com

Optics and Laser Technology, www.elsevier.com

Optics and Lasers in Engineering, www.elsevier.com

Optics Letters, www.ol.osa.org

Optics and Spectroscopy, www.maik.si.ru/journals

Physical Review (American Physical Society),
    www.pra.eps.org

Books

The books that follow will help you increase your understanding of how lasers work and of laser applications in various fields. This list is, of course, not exhaustive. Your reference librarian can help you find other books about lasers. You can also find more books by writing to one of the colleges or universities listed in Chapter 8 and in Appendix B. Address your letter to the dean of the engineering school, the head of the physics department, or a person in a comparable position, and ask him or her to recommend an appropriate reading list.

Beason, Doug. *The E-Bomb: How America's Directed Energy Weapons Will Change the Way Future Wars Will Be Fought.* Cambridge, Mass.: De Capo Press, 2006.

Bromberg, Joan L. *The Laser in America, 1950–1970.* Cambridge, Mass.: MIT Press, 1991.

Brugnera, Aldo. *Atlas of Laser Therapy Applied to Clinical Dentistry*, translated from Portuguese. Lombard, Ill.: Quintessence Publishing Company, 2006.

Harbison, James P. *Lasers: Harnessing the Atom's Light.* New York: Scientific American Library, 1998.

Hecht, Jeff. *The Laser Guidebook*, 2nd ed. Blue Ridge Summit, Pa.: TAB Books, 1999.

———. *Understanding Lasers: An Entry-Level Guide.* New York: IEEE Press, 1994.

Kuhn, Kelin J. *Laser Engineering.* New York: Prentice Hall, 1998.

Lakshminarayanan, Vasudeven, and Kathie Bailey-Mathai. *Optics in the United States.* Washington, DC: National Research Council, 2005.

Laufer, Gabriel. *Introduction to Optics and Lasers in Engineering.*
New York, Cambridge University Press, 1996.

Lauterborn, Werner, and Thomas Kurz. *Coherent Optics:*
Fundamental Applications. New York: Springer Publishing,
1999.

Lenk, John D. *Lenk's Laser Handbook: Featuring CD, CDV, and*
CD-ROM Technology. New York: McGraw-Hill, 1992.

McComb, Gordon. *Lasers, Ray Guns, and Light Cannons: Projects*
from the Wizard's Workbench. New York: McGraw-Hill, 1997.

Silfvast, William T. *Laser Fundamentals.* England: Cambridge
University Press, 1996.

Strategies Unlimited, Fiber and Industrial Lasers Market Review and
Forecast: 2007. Mountain View, Calif.: PennWell, 2007.